# The Afterlife

Conversations with my Guide

Prudence Ann Smith M.D.

Copyright © 2013 Prudence Ann Smith M.D.
All rights reserved.

ISBN: 0615886035
ISBN 13: 9780615886039
Library of Congress Control Number: 2013916823
Belle Publishers, Tulare, CA

# Dedication

*This book is dedicated to my everlasting love, and now my guide, who has transitioned to the other side, and given me the greatest gift I could ever have, the assurance of continued, eternal love, and to all guides, and all beloved souls, in the body or spirit, who have contributed to our journey.*
*This truly is my guide's book, for much of the content is channeled from him, and without having lost and found him, this book would not have been written.*

# Table of Contents

| | | |
|---|---|---|
| Chapter 1 | My Story | 1 |
| Chapter 2 | Becoming a Medium | 11 |
| Chapter 3 | The Process | 21 |
| Chapter 4 | Continuation of Identity | 33 |
| Chapter 5 | The Afterlife-What It Is Like | 39 |
| Chapter 6 | Levels of the Afterlife | 47 |
| Chapter 7 | Reality | 53 |
| Chapter 8 | Right and Wrong | 57 |
| Chapter 9 | Earth Lessons | 61 |
| Chapter 10 | Progression in the Afterlife | 65 |
| Chapter 11 | Fate and Free Will | 71 |
| Checker 12 | Choices in the Afterlife | 73 |
| Chapter 13 | Karma | 77 |
| Chapter 14 | Reincarnation | 81 |
| Chapter 15 | World of Illusion | 85 |
| Chapter 16 | Spirit Body | 89 |
| Chapter 17 | Spirit Senses | 95 |
| Chapter 18 | Sex and Touch | 99 |
| Chapter 19 | Merging | 103 |
| Chapter 20 | Relationships | 109 |
| Chapter 21 | Spirit Occupations and Recreation | 119 |

| Chapter 22 | Love ........................................................................ 123 |
| Chapter 23 | Soulmates and Twin Flames ....................... 127 |
| Chapter 24 | Union ..................................................................... 131 |
| Chapter 25 | Source ................................................................... 135 |
| Chapter 26 | Negative Spirits ........................................... 139 |
| Chapter 27 | Akashic Records .......................................... 145 |
| Chapter 28 | Forgiveness ................................................... 149 |
| Chapter 29 | Heaven ...................................................... 153 |
| Chapter 30 | Paranormal Investigation ........................ 157 |
| Chapter 31 | Memorable Messages ............................... 165 |
| Chapter 32 | Spirit Guidance ............................................ 171 |
| Chapter 33 | Skepticism and Belief ................................ 175 |
| Chapter 34 | War Stories ................................................... 179 |
| Chapter 35 | House Cleansings, Guides, and Déjà Vu ... 189 |
| Chapter 36 | PostScript ................................................ 193 |

One

# My Story

Do you believe in life after death? I do. Most of the great religions of the world teach that there is a life after death but also teach that it is wrong to attempt to communicate with those who have crossed over. No one can conclusively prove our continued existence, but as individuals we can acquire evidence that gives us compelling reason to believe in our continued existence.

I am lucky. When I was young I always pondered the reason for our existence, the meaning of life, and the possibility of eternal life. My grandmother was a medium, not a professional medium, but a reluctant medium, who came by her gift naturally. Of all those in the family, I was the most curious, and I loved to hear her talk about her experiences.

I recall how she went into a trance. While she was in the bed before she fell asleep, she often became paralyzed or catatonic, unable to move, and that is when spirits would come to her. Later she would describe what they looked like or said. She saw them more often then she heard them, mostly not in entirety, but from the waist up. When she heard words it was usually brief. Sometimes she didn't know the spirits, and sometimes she saw a spirit she knew, such as my grandfather.

I have since learned that she was a physical medium and a mental medium, more clairvoyant than clairaudient.

She also had the gift of automatic writing. She would describe feeling a pain in her arm and then feel compelled to write. The handwriting that came through her hand was not her own, but in the unique style of the deceased communicator.

My grandmother never used her gift professionally because of the stigma against mediums. She felt people would call her crazy. I asked her how she first acquired her abilities and she said visits with the afterlife began unsolicited when she was around 16 years of age. She was fearful of what was happening but powerless to prevent it, so she just accepted it.

She described an early experience where she was awakened from sleep and thrown against the wall and bruised, only to discover gas had been escaping in the house. The lives of her and her family had been saved by intervention from the other side. My mother also corroborated this experience.

As a teenager, I purchased many books on telepathy, ESP, and psychic phenomena, quite a few from the Theosophical Society. It was when I was a young adult that I received messages through her for myself. As an only child many of my friends were much older than myself. Several who had passed away came through my grandmother.

The messages that came through were accurate and I knew beyond a doubt they were real. One included the address, place of death, and an informal name my friend always used in addressing me, none of which my grandmother knew. In fact, I remembered the color of the hospital building where he died incorrectly. When I drove by it, I discovered that I was wrong and it was the color my grandmother had seen in her vision. Also, the nickname my friend used to address me was known by no one but myself and my friend. I had never called him from my house where a conversation could have been overheard. I met this friend while in college, never spoke about him with my family, and never called him from my home. There was no way that anyone could have known the private information that came through her.

Another friend who had passed came through in automatic writing. The handwriting was his, with unique characteristics, although my grandmother had never seen his handwriting. He had just passed, and believing in the afterlife, I presumed he was communicating through my grandmother and I began speaking to him in my thoughts. My grandmother didn't know him nor did she know I was mentally speaking to him. While my grandmother was writing, I was mentally asking him a question. My friend's name, the words "love" and "no mourning" came through first. The answer yes came through at the end of her transmitted message. Everything that came through her was appropriate to our relationship. I still have that piece of paper with the automatic writing on it. It was a great gift to know that we survive death. The question I was asking at the end of the communication was if we can be with our loved ones when we pass. Although my grandmother did not know I was asking a question, the answer yes came through at the end of the page.

A friend of mine, who is a phenomenal medium, but works professionally in the medical field and has participated in development circles with me, brought through a relative of mine whom she had never met and never even knew existed. In the reading, she described his dwelling room by room, and accurately identified where everything was located, described his habits, what he liked, where furniture and objects were placed, and how a dog played with him. She correctly identified his birth month, his physical appearance, his on and off mustache, and his religious background. She even confirmed the one disagreement we used to have. He used to feel that communication with the dead was improper. Through her he told me, "I now realize Christianity and spirits can go together." I later took her to see his home, and as she walked through it, she recognized that everything was located exactly where she had seen it in her mediumship reading except for one thing. She walked over to a place in the living room and said "I was wrong about where his chair was because I saw it here." I said, "No, you weren't wrong. Where you're standing is exactly where he always used to sit in his wheelchair." So everything she got was exactly correct.

I used to discuss religion with that relative and speculate on what the afterlife might be like. I laughingly recall what he once said. He remarked, "The afterlife is probably so wonderful that if we really knew what it is like, people would probably be in line to jump off the bridge, pushing others out of the way so that they could jump first." In a mediumship session in which that relative came through since his passing, I asked him, "Is the afterlife like we thought it was?" The answer he gave was, "It is much more beautiful than we ever thought."

I later joined a church and for many years did not pursue any further contact because of the tenets of the church. Then one day something happened that changed my entire life. I lost someone I deeply loved, someone who was my entire world. I needed to know that he heard me, knew how I felt, and that we were in contact. In complete despair I contacted a medium, Robert Brown, who with specific evidence of his survival, reunited us. Robert gave me many evidential details of his personal life, which assured me he was still alive and that I was speaking with him.

I began talking with the love of my life and Robert said he was working hard to manifest himself in the physical. Robert said, "Oh, this is interesting." My loved one was stepping forward to act as my guardian and since has become my guide. I remember being confused by the names and asked him, "Aren't you my soulmate?" He replied, "What difference do names make? Are the two exclusive? Can't I be your guide, your guardian, and your soulmate? No matter what name you use, the love is the same. If I love you forever, it is the relationship that matters, not the name you give it. The love is the same regardless of what name you ascribe to it."

I knew that life continues because of the early experiences I had in my life with my grandmother, but, with the loss of my loved one, I was still inconsolable. I spoke often and fervently to my deceased loved one in my thoughts. He began to communicate with me in dreams. I had multiple vivid dreams in which we were together, some with short conversations or feelings that answered some of the questions I had. They were not like an ordinary dream, but were very clear, very vivid, and I could remember them word for word. They are called visitations.

One day when I was particularly distressed, on my birthday, in fact, I felt him distinctly touching my shoulder. It was unmistakably real. I felt and saw the depression on my arm. I was astonished and knew that it was him. This was a huge turning point for me. It gave me the contentment and consolation that I needed. After that realization that we could be in contact without the help of a medium, I began to meditate and talk to him. Gradually, I started to hear his voice.

I began haltingly to hear phrases of conversation from him. At first they came slowly and briefly, but with time they came fluently. We began to talk frequently, but at times I was troubled with the thought of how to separate his words from my thoughts. I was fearful that what I heard may just be wish fulfillment. I didn't want to influence or color our conversations to reflect my own longings and wishes. I wanted to know as clearly and objectively as possible what he was saying to me.

We began to devise a system of confirmation, in which he would gently move my finger, my arm, or my head. I would actually feel the gentle pull or force of him moving me. Sometimes, alternatively, I could feel him touch my eye lid and make it flutter, or touch a sensory nerve with his electromagnetic energy, and I would feel a very distinct, very focal electrical charge, almost like a twinge or pins and needles sensation inside, not painful, but very definite and forceful. We did this in response to questions I had as confirmation that he was speaking to me and that I was getting the information correctly, that it wasn't my imagination. This "electrical"confirmation was not a random event. It occurred directly in response to my question for confirmation that what I was hearing was accurate. Sometimes he would give me a physical confirmation on his own, and then I would hear his words following.

At one time I obtained the information to download some free software that would allow me to collect EVPS, electronic voice phenomena, myself, and record them. This was done over the background of a frequency sweep of AM radio noise, a home version of the ITC ghost box that paranormal investigators use. I asked questions and obtained responses. Some which were very personal I will not include, but on one where I stated to him, "I won't worry about anything then," the reply instantly came back very clearly, "That's the best." The background radio sweep loops, and when you listen to it, the words, "that's the best", are not there. Those words so clearly heard on the recording afterward were unquestionably from my loved one on the other side.

Only short phrases came through. I understand that for spirits who have crossed over rather than those who choose to remain near the earth plane, commonly regarded as ghosts, it is more difficult to communicate because their vibration is elevated and is farther removed from ours.

As we communicated more and more directly, I obtained corroborating messages from multiple mediums in different geographical areas who didn't know of him, didn't know of our relationship, and didn't know each other. Information of a private, detailed nature was obtained, which could not be obtained from the Internet. Multiple times the exact same statement, word for word, was obtained through these different mediums. This was strong confirmation that I was hearing him accurately and that the information came from him and not from my mind.

Often times to provide further assurance for me he would state something to me in words I hadn't used for years. He would phrase something in a way that was not characteristic of me or use a word that I never used. Sometimes he would say something that was totally unexpected.

Because of his loss and my love for him I began to attend mediumship development retreats and joined a development circle. Not only have I begun to develop abilities of my own, I have learned from losing him things which I would never otherwise have learned. I have learned to forgive all those who have hurt me. I desired to correct my own shortcomings, things that many of us do in our lifetime, lies, cheating, selfishness, justifying our own wrongdoing because others have done us wrong. I desired to live the truths I knew, not just understand and believe them. I wanted to help others who because of a loss felt their life was not worth living. I wanted to try to be a little kinder. I wanted to be a better person.

Now I am in frequent contact with my loved one and know we will be together on the other side. We have made spiritual commitments to each other. Many of the things he has told me, he has confirmed through other mediums as well. I know through this that I am hearing him accurately.

One very specific incident I will recount. One evening I was depressed because I was not able to go to our spirit development circle because of the weather. The road was closed off and I couldn't make the three-hour drive. A friend and I decided to meditate. What came through him was incontrovertible truth of after death communication and one of the most beautiful messages I have ever received. After we finished meditating, I asked my friend if he had heard anything. He said he had heard something crazy that didn't make any sense. He saw two women in a kitchen, one of whom he felt was his guide, and one turned to the other, shrugged her shoulders, and said, "Well, I guess we'll just have to bake an elephant cake." I was astounded. This was something only two of us knew, myself and my deceased loved one. It had a very personal and intimate meaning for myself and my loved one that no one else knew. No one would have guessed something that specific and unique. Hearing that was the best thing that could ever have happened to me. From this I knew that all of my dreams of our union in spirit would come true.

Being without the one I love is the worst thing that I could imagine, but knowing that he is waiting for me on the other side and that we will be together, is the best thing. I am writing this because I want others to know that there is life after death and that they can contact the ones they have loved and lost. I want others to have the same gift of healing I have experienced.

Now I am able to bring through some messages to people I don't know that are specific evidence to them of the survival of friends and loved ones. I take credit for none of this ability. It is a gift from the other side, from guides, loved ones, and, I believe, from God himself. I am very thankful for it and for any way I can give others the comfort I have received.

This is the story of my opening, which is referred to as opening up to the reality of and communication with the other side. This is the evidence that secures my hope of a future fulfillment of my dreams and for a beautiful continuation of existence on the other side of death.

Two

# Becoming a Medium

For anyone who thinks this is impossible, my message to you is that three years ago I thought it was impossible for me, too. Because I was fortunate enough to have had a mediumistic, spiritually gifted grandmother, I had evidential proof when I was young that we continue living after we die, and that there is another "world". But despite my interest, I never dreamed that communication was possible for me and that I also had a gift.

I describe it as a gift because the knowledge that there is a continuation of life and that my loved ones are still alive and connected with me through love is the greatest gift I can imagine. Like any other good thing, mediumship can be abused and misused by those who do not have the highest or best intentions.

That said, my wish is that those who grieve also might know that they too can develop this gift of communication. If I can develop this gift at an older age, I know that there are others who can too. It is built by the bridge of love.

Like any ability or gift, such as playing a musical instrument, writing a book, or understanding mathematics, some will be able to develop this gift more easily than others. But

I will never say that it cannot be developed. If I can come as far as I have come, I wish to encourage others who have lost a loved one through death to work at developing their own personal communication.

We never know what is possible until we try. If you seek to do this, I recommend you always ask for protection from God or Source, that you pray or surround yourself with the white light of godly protection before you proceed in order to protect yourself from negative influences. As there are negative people on this earth and you would not leave the door of your home open for malefactors to come in and rob you, so too your mind and soul should be protected before spirit communication.

The initial stages of becoming a medium are what is referred to as "opening up". There are many people who demonstrate mediumistic abilities naturally, early in life, without seeking them. My grandmother was such a medium. She began having unsolicited experiences, and therefore, sometimes puzzling or frightening experiences, at the age of 16.

There are others like myself, who, because of a devastating loss and grief, seek confirmation of a loved one's continued existence, and discover through a deep emotional need that we, too, can develop mediumistic abilities.

What I learned in this case, is that you first have to believe that another life exists and that communication is possible. I began by speaking often and fervently to my loved one. Subsequently, I began to hear his words in my mind. I knew that I did not "think" some of the things I heard. He then began to give me physical confirmations that it was indeed him speaking, and not my imagination, or wish fulfillment. Sometimes he would give me an unusual word that I had not used in years, or say something completely unexpected. In this manner I knew that he truly was speaking to me.

I also have had corroboration when the exact same words, a specific sentence, came through several different mediums in different states who didn't even know each other. Another medium drew a "spirit portrait" of my loved one which was a very authentic replica, having never seen him nor known of his identity.

Many personal verifications have come through to me that are personal statements/confirmations of things that would never be found on the Internet. One such transmission was something so personal that only the deceased person and I had knowledge of it.

The well-known medium, John Edward, was a guest lecturer at one of the conferences I attended in the Bahamas. He said that when he was in the early stages of development, he, too, was reluctant to communicate with his own mother because he questioned the objectivity of the message he was getting. This is a common problem many mediums experience when communicating with their own loved ones. I always question myself, but the above methods, worked out between my loved one and myself, have helped to assure me of the validity of the communications.

I joined a spirit circle, a development circle or group, of about ten people who meet two-four times a month. We open up by asking for protection and stating an opening prayer. We then ground ourselves and begin with a meditation and an opening exercise for opening our energy centers or chakras. We then ask our spirit guides to bring through spirits with messages for loved ones, visiting sitters, or group members.

I brought along a friend who early in life had a near death experience. He was in a coma for several months and officially died, with no cardiac activity, but was brought back to life. He described his near death experience to me. He said that he suddenly found himself pain free and floating above his bed in the corner of the room. He looked down on his own body and realized that he was dead. That was when the thought occurred to him, without any emotional distress, "Well, if this is the time, then this is the time."

He could see and hear all of the proceedings, even when the doctor literally kicked the nurse in the back side to get her to hurry and retrieve the needed "crash cart ". When he was resuscitated after the incident, he says the doctor turned white as a sheet when he recounted to him in detail what had happened while he was "dead".

Before the near death episode, while he was in a coma for several months, he had a visit from an uncle. He said it was very comforting and his uncle reassured him that he shouldn't worry, he would recover. Later, when he did recover, he told his mother about the visit and his mother got a peculiar look on her face. She later told him that the uncle who had visited him while he was in the coma had died several weeks before.

As he went to circle meetings, he, too, began to develop mediumship and was able to deliver accurate and evidential messages to others. One example of the sudden development of his astounding ability was demonstrated in a teaching exercise devised by the medium Robert Brown, in his Bahamas retreat. He sent Harvey outside of the room and told the group he was selecting three people and he wanted each of those three to choose one deceased person they wanted to hear from. When my friend came back in the room, he was told to go to three people he felt drawn to and give each one a message from a loved one. There were about fifteen people in the group. Not only did he go to the correct three people, he went to them in order, and if that wasn't enough, got the correct spirit that each one had chosen while he was out of the building, and delivered the message.

I think everyone was shocked. I know I was. I asked him how he did it, and he said he didn't know, that when he delivers messages like that, the information just "flows" into his mind and he feels "zoned out", which I believe is a light trance state.

No one can "know" the truth of this work unless they experience it for themselves. This same friend worked with a man who had recently lost his wife and was grieving. My friend told him to be silent, to meditate and speak to his wife in his thoughts. The man began to have dreams in which his wife communicated with him and now has an open channel of communication.

Several other noteworthy episodes occurred with my friend. In one episode, a medium from the group named Peter asked me for my advice on what avenue he should pursue for his continued development. I told him that I felt I was biased and couldn't give him an objective answer. So I came up with a solution. I told my friend, I am going to ask you for two answers, but I'm not going to give you the questions. I just want you to channel the answers you hear from your guides. He actually got some answers that made sense. One of them was that Peter didn't need to go to a training session (he was contemplating going overseas for training), and that he should start teaching. Peter actually followed that advice from Spirit.

Here is another occurrence that was interesting regarding my friend. We were all involved in a teaching exercise devised by "Mama Elle", a visiting medium and teacher, in the Bahamas. She had brought along her "psi" cards, a set of cards similar to, but also different from, Tarot cards. She had half of the group each read 3 cards selected by a member of the other half, who stood behind one of the readers and could not be seen. My friend started giving a reading based on the cards. He didn't know that Mama Elle was chosen to stand behind him. After he gave her correct information in his reading, she stopped him and said, "How long have you been reading psi cards "? He looked at his watch and said, "About 5 minutes." He didn't know that he was supposed to let her ask questions first. He gave the answers before he got the questions.

If you desire to know for yourself, sit and meditate. Protect yourself with a prayer or the white light of God and ask for guidance. Do this on a regular basis and you may be able to develop mediumship.

One thing that I have learned since pursuing this interest is that there are many good mediums whose names are not in the spotlight. One of these individuals had possessed this ability since childhood. Several others had developed it in later years as a response to the particularly painful loss of a loved one. Several are also physical mediums, who can produce physical phenomena such as table movement, deflection of a compass needle, automatic writing, trance-channeling, movement of the planchette on a Ouija board, and spiritually directed artwork/portraits.

I had always heard about the table movement or "table tipping "described in some of the pioneering books of spiritualism, but I had never seen it. I believed it could happen but always wanted to witness it for myself. One day I did.

I was amazed to see a table move under its own power, "spirit power" as it turned and moved rapidly across the floor at a development session in the Bahamas. It was a table that was brought in off the porch of a restaurant by us and not rigged in any way. It's one of those cases where you have to see it to believe it. This happened in broad daylight with some of my friends positioned around the table and touching the top very lightly with fingertips only, not the palms of their hands or thumbs, and not enough to move the heavy table rapidly. One participant videotaped it on her smart phone. All of us were so excited we started shouting, "Turn, baby, turn ". It was something I'll never forget. I had never actually seen this before, but now I know it exists. I was awed and delighted at yet another proof that Spirit is real.

I was present at a different type of physical mediumship event another time. This one was performed in complete darkness and participants were searched before entering the room. The people who put on the event even used metal detectors to search us, and we had to empty our pockets and remove our belts and shoes. We could have passed inspection at the airport. Physical mediums reportedly can be harmed by loose objects in the room, as they supposedly secrete ectoplasm from their bodies, a substance used by spirits to manifest themselves. Although the presenting mediums involved were good mental mediums and gave many good evidential messages with personal details no one could obtain through any public search means such as the Internet, the physical session was a disappointment to me, as the situation was set up so that there was no means that anyone in audience could prove that any of the supposed phenomena were real.

I will never attend a physical seance again unless it is performed in red light where I can observe the phenomena and decide for myself if they are "real ". I have spoken since that time with several other excellent mediums and channelers I respect, who also feel the same way I do. If you are placed in a position where you cannot judge for yourself whether something is real or not, why attend and spend the money?

Several of the mediums with whom I've sat in development circles are also involved in writing books. I'm sure each one will provide a different individual glimpse into what they have learned through their experiences.

Several of them channel individual spirits as well as inspirational messages from collectives or groups of advanced souls such as the soul groups calling themselves Abraham and Silver. I have heard some of the messages and find them inspiring and beautiful. It is interesting to me that when I was studying in school I learned of the debate about the authorship of several of Shakespeare's works. Some people felt that several of them may have been penned by another writer, possibly Sir Francis Bacon. The general conclusion was that they were consistent with the style of Shakespeare and therefore felt to likely represent his works. In this same way, I became able to identify the source or soul group that had delivered a particular message based upon the syntax and style of writing, as well as the type of content. Each group had a distinctive subject matter and delivery.

I am told that we all possess a certain amount of this ability to contact the spirit realm and those who have crossed over to some extent, and as with any ability, we can improve it if we seek it and practice it.

I often ask myself, how do I know that this is real, how do I know that this is accurate? How can I tell that what I am hearing are the words of my deceased loved one rather than my own words or thoughts, something I have originated? How can I be more objective in the message I receive or deliver, and less subjective?

Many mediums have given me messages. The private details they have given me are nothing that could have been obtained from the Internet or the public records. They consist of much more than names, dates, and causes of death. They also included very private details, some so private that only two of us, myself and the deceased person, even knew of those statements/occurrences and facts. One was the message a friend gave me that I described earlier. The words were "I guess we'll just to bake an elephant cake". How would anyone guess something that bizarre and particular?

Another young medium, naturally gifted, brought through a message from my mother so accurate in its emotional content and private detail, much of which wasn't even known by the rest of the family, that it felt as though my mother was standing right next to me, speaking to me. My grandmother's automatic writing included a message for me from a deceased friend. It was in his handwriting, not hers, with specific idiosyncrasies that were uniquely characteristic of the way he wrote. My grandmother had never even seen his writing.

Another way that I know the communication is real is due to the fact that I can feel my loved one's touch, an electromagnetic, tingling sensation. I also was touched once on the shoulder so firmly that I could see the movement of my skin and soft tissues. Sometimes I feel the force of him moving my hand, arm, or head. At other times I feel a neural tingling sensation, like the ones people have when they are being tested for muscle innervation. These are not random but occur simultaneously with answers that I am hearing to my questions. They are very specific physical confirmation that I am hearing the answers and receiving them accurately.

Three

# The Process

I was given a lesson about how difficult it is to identify people. In one of our development circles a message came through that was directed at me. I was given information that was true or could have pertained to several people in my life-several with similar personality characteristics. Then there were several details given that only pertained to one person. One detail could have been interpreted symbolically or literally and if taken symbolically, could have been applied to several people, but if taken literally, could have identified only one person. But one detail was given that could only have been true for one person and it was a very significant personal detail. Therefore, I was able to connect the reading with only one individual. As I have personally been in contact with the person you may ask why he came through another medium at the circle. This is because it is a teaching circle and we are trying to become better mediums and to analyze how to get clearer detail and to give messages in a more evidential manner.

Sometimes several spirits will come through at once, giving separate details simultaneously. This is also a teaching point that the medium must ask one to step aside momentarily so they can separate the confirmations and the sitter will not be confused. There was one detail that came through the reading that puzzled me. I directly asked my loved one about it and he said the detail could be subjectively interpreted differently as the medium chose a word from her own vocabulary that gave a different connotation to the meaning he was attempting to communicate. That was another teaching lesson. The medium was very good but just think of the telephone game some of us played as kids-how difficult it is to relay a message we hear with our physical ears. How much more difficult is it to get an exact message when it is filtered through the mind of the medium who could possibly add his or her own personal coloration or subjective feeling to the message just by their choice of words. It is easy to add words that convey a different meaning than what the spirit intended. For instance, a medium might use the word workaholic to describe a spirit, when perhaps they had to work very hard because of circumstances, but were not inherently a self-driven workaholic.

So no message or medium is 100% perfect or accurate. I am not perfect and I don't know anyone else who is, so all we can do is strive to be as accurate as we can.

Another exercise we practiced in the Bahamas was attempting to collect as much information from the spirit as we could using just one sense-clairaudience-spoken or heard words, clairvoyance-visual images or pictures, or clairsentience-conveyed feelings or sensations. Some of us are more visual, some more verbal, some more intuitive. So if we exercise each mental faculty as we would a body part we develop the whole and become better communicators then we would be if we only used one method of conveying a message.

One of the mediums in training was given the assignment of standing up on the platform and giving a message from a spirit using only the sense of clairsentience. Most of us use all three senses in varying degrees when we communicate. But each of us usually has one sense that is dominant and like a muscle that is weak, the other senses can be developed with exercise.

The medium got up and started delivering the message strictly from the sense of feeling. That's quite a handicap, as she couldn't use anything she saw or heard. I thought the message was for me, but one thing didn't fit. She said the spirit felt like a male-in other words, a strong, dominant personality. Finally she said something that cinched it. She said, "I feel that my eyes are bothering me. They hurt and I can't see properly. I keep wanting to rub them". That was the last piece of the puzzle. My mother passed in the ICU on a ventilator, in a coma- like state, from a complication of the chemotherapy she had for pancreatic cancer. She had a severe problem with her eyes. She couldn't close or move them and she had to receive applications of eye lubricant drops to keep her eyes moist. It must have been quite painful.

The only detail that didn't fit was the medium's feeling of a male spirit. But my mother had a very strong, dominant personality, one that would not be described as feminine. That explains why the medium interpreted my mother's personality as male. This demonstrates the difficulty mediums have if they only use one of their senses. If she had been able to use her visual clairvoyance, she would have known my mother was a female with a strong personality.

A different exercise given by another medium, James Van Praagh, illustrates this same point. He had two mediums work together, one sitting in a chair and reading the other medium, who stood behind the back of the chair, where he couldn't be seen. It was an exercise in psychic reading.

The one detail that the reading medium most often got wrong was gender. The male/female distinction seemed to be the most difficult piece of information to discern. That makes sense, because information from the Other Side indicates that spirits have no fixed gender, and most of us have had incarnations as both males and females.

If we use all our senses to describe an event how much more colorful it is. If someone is deaf or blind and lacks sensation how much more difficult it is for them to communicate because they are limited to the other senses in their description and explanation. So as mediums we are more thorough and more descriptive when we learn to develop all of our senses for communication. Say what we are hearing, seeing, and feeling.

Getting names and numbers is difficult for most people. Conveying a thought seems easier. Some mediums are better at this than others, but details are more difficult to get than emotions or general characteristics. Each of us has our own strengths, as some people find dancing or music, a sport or intellectual pursuit like science, easier to learn based on their own inherent talent. But exact names seem more difficult for most. I have seen some astonishing mediums who get them better than others but most struggle with this. As with any talent, it can be strengthened, improved, and developed.

A medium I met in the Bahamas who was famous for her Zumba lessons and was incredibly physically fit, employed a system for obtaining information such as relationships, names, numbers, and cause of death.

For relationships, she pictured the communicating spirit standing above, beside, or below the sitter. This is similar to the system John Edwards uses. Above signified those in the parents' or grandparents' generations; beside, or the same level, siblings, cousins, or friends; below, children, grandchildren, pets, or youngsters.

For names, she pictured the alphabet strung out linearly in front of her and asked the spirit to highlight a particular letter.

For numbers, she would picture a clock face and asked the spirit to move the clock hand to a particular number.

For cause of death, she assigned the numbers 1 through 4 for the main causes of death-illness, accident, suicide, and homicide. You can also ask the spirit to point to or make a black mark on the part of the body that caused their death.

For determining geographic location, you can ask a spirit to put a pin on an image of the map.

These methods are all helpful for those mediums who are predominantly clairvoyant and depend on their sense of vision.

For those who are clairsentient, or depend on feelings, the spirit can often make the medium feel what they were feeling at the time of their death, such as stomach pain, chest pain, dizziness, shortness of breath, etc.

As in any endeavor, we need to protect ourselves. Just as we place burglar alarms and locks on our homes and cars, we also need protection for ourselves, physically and psychologically or spiritually. Just as there are people in life who would do us harm, there are spirits who have passed from this life who would also seek to do us harm.

Spirits do not become instantly perfect when they transition from the human state to the spirit state. Some who cross over into the light improve or learn, but this is not an instant process. Those who were negative and conducted a negative and malicious or harmful life deliberately, do not move to the same vibrational level in the next life as those who were kind and helpful. Here on earth all levels of development coexist, but after death we graduate to the level of spiritual development we have achieved in life. Some spirits remain near the earth plane for unfinished business, for revenge, anger, love of a place or person, or for prolonged and prevailing earthly desires.

That is why we also begin our circles with an intention of giving messages in the interest of the highest and greatest good for all present, in the spirit of love, and we ask for protection from our spirit guides, loved ones in spirit, and from God, or Source, whatever name we choose for the greater power that governs the universe and all in it.

That is why undisciplined connection with the spirit world can be dangerous. Using tools of communication such as Ouija boards, divining or dowsing rods, or seances can open you to communication with a negative spirit, as indiscriminately allowing anyone off the street to walk into your home can result in robbery, violence, or murder.

That is why it is so important if you seek communication with the spirit realm to protect yourself by a prayer and setting the intention of love, by asking for the white light of God to surround you or for protection from the Great Spirit that some call God.

I once experienced a reading in the Bahamas on the difficulty of identifying a spirit in a large audience because of the common experiences and personality traits we all share. The medium on the platform was very good and gave one characteristic after another about the spirit. As he went on, the audience was asked to raise their hand if they could identify with what was said and thought the spirit was for them. It was amazing to me how many hands went up. There must have been twenty. The medium struggled to get more information. As he proceeded with each additional piece of information a hand or 2 went down as possibilities were eliminated.

Eventually, in this painful process, there were only several hands left. This was a teaching session conducted by Spirit to show us how many things we have in common and how difficult it can be to identify one specific spirit out of many. Finally only two hands were left up and at last the spirit gave a detail that was so specific it could only apply to one person. The medium got a street name of residence- Oak. That finally identified the spirit conclusively.

That is why when I give a reading I always include one question when I ask the spirits for information. I always say, "Can you give me one piece of information, one incident, possession, or memory that the sitter can identify with that will let them know this is specifically you, that is unique to your memories together or your relationship"?

Let me give you an example. Once I was giving a reading in the Bahamas and I was getting some information. As I gave each piece to the sitter she agreed but said, "Well, that is kind of general, I need something more to be sure it's who I think it is." I finally said to the spirit, "Please help me, give me one thing so personal and specific that the sitter will know for certain that it's you."

So what did the spirit do? They sneezed. I thought, "Aw, oh, here is where I'm really going to look like a fool." So I always heard give what you get-don't judge or interpret-just trust. So I did. And she said, "Oh, now I know its him. Every time he went out into the sun he used to sneeze. No one else I knew did that." So there you have it. Sometimes the most trivial piece of information that you feel foolish for giving identifies the spirit exclusively for the person receiving the message.

Speaking of, "give what you get," there is the instance I mentioned before. One night we had bad winter weather. We had to make a three hour drive on the highway to get to Los

Angeles for spirit development circle. The pass in the mountains was closed and we couldn't go. I had so looked forward to the learning experience and mingling with friends and passed loved ones that I became depressed. A friend who also lived in my town said, "Well, let's sit and meditate by ourselves and see if we get any messages." Both of us were novices and didn't know what to expect. We got through meditating and I said, "Well, did you get anything?" The most wonderful cryptic personal message came through. He said, "Well, I got something but it's crazy and doesn't make any sense to me." I said, "Well, tell me anyway."

He said, "Well, I saw two women standing in a kitchen. One looked like the chef, Julia Childs. One turned to the other, threw up her hands, and said, "Well, I guess we're just going to have to bake an elephant cake." Then they walked out of the kitchen and that was it. He felt foolish giving me the message. Well, this was the most personal, beautiful message I could ever have received. That had a very personal meaning for me, shared only by myself and my loved one in spirit as a very intimate, precious detail. I was ecstatic because it let me know something I needed to know deeply in my soul. It is private, and one of the most beautiful, healing messages of all the beautiful healing messages I have ever received-specifically, because it was known to no one but the deceased person and myself. And it was not a detail any one would ever have guessed.

If you question whether I was read psychically or telepathically, I'll tell you that I have received other messages, some about things that I didn't even know but had to find out in retrospect.

This is the message I received through my grandmother, who was a natural, but not a professional medium. A message she obtained through automatic writing referenced the "pet" name or familiar name a friend used to address me. No one living knew that name he called me, and my grandmother had never met him or known him personally. She also described the hospital where he had died. Interestingly enough, I had incorrectly remembered it as being one color, and when I went to check, discovered I had remembered it incorrectly and indeed, it was the color she had stated.

In another communication, I also had warnings through her of some danger or future event I needed to avoid that was unknown to me at the time, and later found out the event and circumstances could have happened. I was spared a devastating trauma by heeding her advice, conveyed from the spirit world by my loved ones.

When my mother was young I remember her telling me a story about an incident that happened at her home. The family was sleeping at home in bed at night and, unknown to them, a gas leak had developed in the house and all were in danger of dying. My grandmother, who was also asleep, was shoved so forcefully against the wall she awoke and later developed bruises from the incident. She discovered the gas leak and the family was saved.

Later, when my mother passed, and before I had developed the ability to hear the deceased spirits, she made her presence known to a close relative by turning a light on that was turned off. This happened several times. Why the relative and not me? - Because he was skeptical and didn't look for communication. He was able to describe it objectively, where I would have questioned whether it was my imagination.

Later on, in the Bahamas, my mother came through to me through a young, beginning female medium who was incredibly talented. She was like a young John Edward and gave me such lengthy personal details, both good and bad, about my early relationship with my mother that it was as if my mother were standing in the room telling me these things herself. They were highly personal, intimate and confidential, as well as specific, details of our relationship that no one else knew. I wish I were as talented as that young medium. What a healing gift she has to give to the world.

I believe we all have this ability to varying extents, and, like any other ability, with serious dedication and practice, can improve and develop. An accomplished medium, Kim Russo, commented on a television show, "You need to trust. The biggest mistake people make is not trusting what they've heard, what they know." Also, she said, "It takes a lot of energy to communicate-we have to raise our energy and level of vibration and they have to lower theirs."

My grandmother illustrated this concept when she told me about a spirit communication she had received. She said a spirit had come to her and repeated the name "Charlie Jones, Charlie Jones . It is so difficult to come back." She said, "Oh, that must be my childhood best friend, Charlotte Jones." This communication demonstrates how difficult it is to get names exactly, and, indeed, how difficult it is for those who have passed to overcome the vibrational barrier and manifest themselves to us.

Due to the lack of development circles in my area and the difficulty of making the 6 hour round trip drive to the nearest circle, several friends and I decided to get together on SKYPE. At first we didn't know how it would turn out, but it ended up being quite a success. We were able to bring through spirits as easily as if we were in a room together. This makes sense because time and distance are not significant obstacles in the spirit world.

Spirits can communicate in many different ways. They can communicate with words, feelings, images, songs, and even sometimes smells or tastes. There was, however, one unique reading given by one of my friends at the circle. She started to do automatic writing. The spirit communicated full sentences to her, which she transcribed onto paper. This is how many books have been written in the last century, with spirits communicating their thoughts, ideas, and feelings to someone through automatic writing. A lot of detail can be communicated in this manner. It seems, though, that this is a unique gift that only some mediums demonstrate. Likewise, this type of communication can only be performed by some spirits who are particularly adept at it.

The closer the match between the emotional and intellectual makeup of the spirit and the medium, the closer their vibrational level, and the more similar their gifts are, the clearer and better the communication.

One further incident I will mention because I was the medium "getting the heat". Six of us were participating in a Skype circle when I happened to put out the intention to the spirit world that I needed practice. What happened next was an example of, "Be careful of what you wish for, because you just might get it." I started giving details, one after another, about the personal habits of the communicating spirit. Several of the participants of the circle each said the details could match several spirits they knew. This went on for a half hour with me "sweating bullets", trying to get one detail that would clearly identify who was speaking to us.

It turned out that all four of the spirits shared many similarities and interests and I was getting a mother and grandmother for each of the two sitters. The more details I gave, the more each sitter affirmed, "yes, yes, yes." Finally I got some information about different ages of death and an initial. I had more than one spirit and I was being given an unforgettable lesson in evidential mediumship.

In fact, I heard my guide, who has a great sense of humor, say, "So you want to be a medium." I got the point. You can work ever so hard, but without that evidential detail, name, age of death, number and gender of children, etc., a reading that seems specific to you may pertain to more than one spirit for the sitter. My work is cut out for me.

Four

# Continuation of Identity

When I went to Robert Brown for my first reading, the loved one I was trying to contact stepped forward, and Robert said, "Oh, he says that he is stepping forward to become your guardian." Since that time he is also serving as my guide. When I refer to my guide, I am referring to him. I have decided to withhold his name out of respect for surviving family members who may not share my opinions or experiences.

In Shanna Spalding St. Clair's book, "*Karma I and II*", she channels several advanced spirits, who state, "Consciousness of the spirit is continual (49). The characteristic of any light body is that it will retain complete memory of its cumulative experiences (61). Without perception there would be no existence or purpose (64)." L. Kelway-Bamber, in "*Claude's Second Book*", channels Claude, "Personality is the child of spirit and body and the result of their union is never lost (102)."

My guide states,

> "If we have many lifetimes and assume many identities, what part of us is preserved eternally and what part is temporary?
>
> All of our lifetimes influence our character and we are the sum total of all that we have learned from our individual experiences. What we carry with us is our personality, our individual essence, traits and character, everything that is inside, that we have internalized. Our basic distinguishing characteristics, interests, nature, preferences, and predilections remain.
>
> What we lose is everything that originates from outside, our physical appearance in any given lifetime, accent, language, cultural mores and ideology, and our socially imprinted behavior and customs.
>
> We are not just what we are in one lifetime. We are much more. We are always learning. We are changed by a given lifetime. We are always improving. We are the summation of all of our experiences. We have different costumes and exteriors, different occupations, appearances, and customs. But we are the same person underneath, with the same intellect, emotional nature, spiritual character, and personality/identity. We are influenced by our surroundings and life path. We are a unique personality/intelligence, developing and growing because of our experiences.
>
> When we cross over, we have personalities that are the same. We keep our personal traits and personal identity.
>
> We don't need to keep the negative emotions such as fear, hate, anger, or unhappiness. We can

keep emotions if we choose to. We keep love, kindness, compassion, joy, peace, contentment, excitement, interest, intelligence, curiosity, caring, warmth, happiness, passion, or a deep emotional feeling for someone, affection, desire to be close with someone, devotion, understanding, ecstatic excitement, and deep love."

As Charlotte Dresser states in her book, *"Life Here and Hereafter"*, communicated through automatic writing, "Personality, which is retained, includes the way we look at things, tastes, preferences, and desires (39-41)."

Gretchen Vogel states in her book on the afterlife, *"Choices in the Afterlife"*, "Personality, which is retained, includes all those qualities that form an individual character- attitudes, priorities, interests, traits, and preferences (26, 31)." "The afterlife is a completely self-directed mental and spiritual reality (230)."

My guide states,

> "We do retain our earthly personalities, but are changed by what we learn. I am a little bit kinder, more caring, and more loving, as a result of what I have learned. We still retain character flaws, defects, and weaknesses. Some of us are more changed and some less changed when we cross over. I am more or less similar to the way I was, but I have more understanding.
> We retain our core personality, our essence, through many lifetimes, on the other side, but we learn from our experiences when we can see the bigger picture on the other side. We become a little bit

wiser and grow spiritually from our experiences and the life review we undergo on the other side."

Another channeled message states that we retain repulsion or affection for things and people we disliked or who were dear to us. We retain our idiosyncrasies and emotional memories. Affection, love, or intense interest bridges the chasm. We are all distinct but influenced by others in our community.

In Geraldine Cummin's book, "*The Road to Immortality*", F.W.H. Myers channels, "So many of the dead who endeavor to send messages descriptive of their surroundings and of their life to human beings can only describe the actual appearance of the things about them, can only write from out of that limited personality which they brought with them from the earth (21-22)."

A friend who is a medium uses the pseudonym Karuna. She says that we have other names or vibrational signatures on the other side which are characteristically ours and identify us to other souls. We can use a name from a favorite incarnation if we wish.

My guide explains that we have identifying vibrational signatures which have been ours since our inception. We use our earth names when we are communicating with loved ones left behind.

I have been told by my guide that the negatives we have in our earthly lives are not present on the other side. The negative emotions such as fear, anger, hatred, sadness, and pain, do not exist where he is. They are not needed. He states,

> "We work at what we love and stay with who we love. No one works for a living or is forced to stay with someone with whom they are incompatible. There is

no need for money. The earthly roles of childbearing, raising children, providing for or supporting a family, and housework are no longer relevant. No one can lie, cheat, steal, harm, or kill. Feelings become more intense but are positive. We enjoy companionship and deep eternal love."

Five

# The Afterlife-What It Is Like

In her book, "*Choices in the Afterlife,*" Gretchen Vogel says that the afterlife is a self directed mental and spiritual reality. In other words, we create our own reality in the afterlife. How we think and what we believe to be true influences what we experience. We project and create our own reality. Thoughts become things in the afterlife. Just as anything a man builds on the earth starts with a mental concept and then is executed using the physical materials available to us, in the afterlife thoughts directly fashion or shape the surrounding reality. The environments in the spirit world are as real to their inhabitants as our earthly world is to us.

My guide says,

"We create many things with our thoughts. We have so many choices. None of us has the same way of looking at things. We have very different places we live and different surroundings. There are even more choices then we had on earth. We can create a scenario and live in that scenario. We can create the conditions we want. We learn to control our minds for with our thoughts we create our reality. The Spirit world is not entirely different because we still have our identity, we still have work and recreation."

The medium, Laurie, channels her guides, "There are multiple realities. It depends on where you are. Your beliefs determine your reality. Other times there is a shared common reality."

My guide explains,

"There are many different environments that spirits create on the other side with their thoughts. The finer substance of the other side is more malleable than our physical substance and is responsive to our thoughts. Where a building in the physical world begins as a thought in the mind of the architect and is executed by architectural designs and builders, a building on the other side is created by thought. Many things do not require an intermediary but are created directly.

We create our own reality, and frequently we do it as a joint effort. We often have groups we gravitate to with similar wishes and ideals. So we all make our own life to an extent within the limitations of our level of spiritual development. We are not just recreating a memory, we are creating a new experience through our thoughts.

There is no limit to what we can make with our thoughts provided it does not violate the laws of life. Thought and intention can become solid.

Time is not perceived in the same manner as it is on earth. In a sense, time doesn't exist for us because we do not have the reminiscences of time- there are no work hours or schedules, no need to sleep, no lightness and darkness, no calendars or demarcations of days and years, no aging, sickness, or decay, no seasons, no fatigue or exhaustion. Time is not of importance to us as it was on earth as we do not measure our lives in months or years or experience seasons or the changes of aging and death. We do, however, have a sense of future and past. We can look at the past, present, and with limitations, the future. We have the understanding of the concept of eternity."

I heard one medium in training state that the past, present, and future all exist simultaneously in the afterlife, that time is non-linear. That leads me to ask the question, "If the past, present, and future all exist at the same time, can we go back into our past life and relive it or change the things we did wrong"? That didn't seem right to me, so I asked another medium friend what her take was on that issue. She channeled her guides, indicating that, no, we cannot go back and change the things we did wrong or relive our past life because that would affect everyone else we interacted with and change their lives too. We can evaluate our past life and conjecture what we should have done or would have done if we could go back and live our life over. We can also forgive others who have done us harm and ask others for forgiveness for things we have done wrong. In that way, we can balance our karma.

My guide indicates,

> "Motion and travel are different. We can simulate walking if we want, but can float or travel nearly

instantaneously through the control of our thoughts and desires. Intention results in action. We merely think and almost immediately are at our destination. We do retain concepts of far and near. We are able to travel.

There is no need for money or property. We do not need to work for dwellings or sustenance as on the earth but work at things we love to do. We do not have to worry about maintaining our bodies or homes. We don't need to worry about illness or crime. We do not have the traditional or customary roles a husband and wife play on earth. There is no need to earn a living or support a family. There is no need to clean or maintain a household or raise children. We are not compelled to stay in an unhappy relationship. Groups and relationships are formed by those whose character and tastes are akin. Affinity is a stronger bond then blood.

There is no need for jealousy because there is no deceit, lying, or cheating. We are not bound in an unhappy relationship. Those who do not mutually love one another do not remain together. We remain together by mutual agreement.

There is no need for possessiveness because we cannot control another soul. We do not remain in a relationship that is not mutual. We depart amicably. Those who share a deep bond of love and affection remain together.

Even when we are not compatible with another soul we maintain respect for their choices, and treat them with kindness, consideration, and compassion.

We communicate with our thoughts and have spirit senses that enable us to hear, see, and feel. We do not need the intermediary sense organs that our physical bodies have. We perceive things directly, not through the mediation of sense organs.

Individuals retain their character. The superficialities of earthly life fall away and we know and are known as we truly are. We cannot lie or hide our true nature and character.

We can have nature and buildings if we want them. We have a physical appearing reality around us not made of the same substance as the earthly realm. We can have a home or personal place of rest if we wish to have one. "

Charlotte Dresser, in her book, "*Spirit World and Spirit Life,*" states that our homes are fit to our personalities (loc 1191, Kindle edition). We are able to create dwellings for our personal privacy but do not need to eat or sleep and as such do not need to spend time in them as on the earth.

My guide indicates,

"Our bodies are of a finer material and higher vibration than the physical earthly bodies we had. We do have form. However, our form is more malleable than that of our former body. We essentially are a discrete collection of energy. With our thoughts and intentions we can present our energy as a ball of light, a cloud, a mist, an orb, or a humanoid type form. We can create bodies for ourselves that are similar to our former earthly bodies but without the internal organs and functions. If we assume a physical type of form we also assume clothing. Although spirits do not have a gender, we can continue to see ourselves as men or women if we like.

We do not age or become sick. There is no need to eat or sleep. We do take short periods of time to renew our energy and relax and rest. We have some recreations similar to those on earth. We were more restricted on earth. We have many intellectual and creative pursuits. We enjoy learning and helping others to learn. We have the opportunity to live out those things we wanted to do but didn't have the opportunity to do on earth. We have counselors, guides, and teachers.

There are higher powers that organize our life. It is not arbitrary, but is controlled and directed."

My guide comments,

"When I crossed over I tried to learn about my life, find out what I did wrong and what I needed to learn from my life. The change was not that difficult. I didn't feel too different. The most difficult part was not knowing what to expect. After I passed the most difficult part was not being able to tell people on earth I was still alive. I tried to progress, made friends, and travelled. I thought the other side was much different from what it is. I think it is similar to what my life on earth was, only much better. My ideas of what life was like before I passed were guided by the Bible. We are not too much different from what we were on earth. I think we are much better off now."

I have been told that we "create our own truth" within the framework of eternal or spiritual law, which is the counterpart to our natural law. We will go to an area or environment in the afterlife with those who are like-minded, with whom we have an affinity and we are together with those with whom we have a bond of love. One medium I know said you and your soulmate or partner are co-creating your life together with your thoughts.

Communication can be difficult with the other side and love is the bridge. Those on the other side have to lower their vibration and we have to raise ours. We can raise our vibration by meditation , prayer, positive thinking, love, and a joyful and grateful attitude.

Spirits progress through many levels of development on the other side, many different levels of increasing vibration and advancement. Spirits are clothed with multiple bodies. These have variously been referred to in the literature as astral, mental, and etheric bodies or energy sheaths, with the pure energy Spirit as the true essential and eternal core. With each successive level we shed the coarser body, and inhabit a less material body.

The many levels of the afterlife are like ascending steps of energy, increasing vibration, and advancing spiritual development. They represent decreasing density. The levels that are closer to our earth plane resemble the reality we know more closely. One of the planes referred to in books and by F.W.H. Myers has been called the plane of illusion. On this plane the environment is created or constructed by thought projections of the Spirit inhabitants, who create their own version of heaven and complete or fulfill the dreams they did not fulfill on earth. This is where each soul can find his or her own truth.

Shanna Spalding St. Clair's book, "*Karma I and II*," states that, "We each began our soul journey with a God given purpose or intent (50)."

My guide states,

> "We are always around you. We don't exist in some distant dimension. We merely exist at a vibrational

level that is ordinarily not perceived on earth. We want you to know the truth about life after death. We try to communicate with you and sometimes we are able to do it. Love is the energy that bridges the gap between our two worlds. Trust is vital in establishing the flow of communication. We are aware of what is occurring in your life and remain connected with you. Those souls you are close to may come to greet you when it is your time to transition."

Six

# Levels of the Afterlife

The transition called death does not instantly confer perfection upon those who have crossed over. Souls do not instantly become perfect at the point of death. Life is like the schoolhouse where we learn lessons that enable us to become a little wiser and better. What we learn from our lives permits us to develop and advance. The medium, Kim Russo, stated that, "Just because you die doesn't mean you're good. When we elevate into the next dimension we are at different levels of development. There are positive and negative spirits in the next dimension."

Charlotte Dresser, in her book, "*Life Here and Hereafter*", states, "Your thought brings you the truth that appeals to you. Heaven is an unlimited space and there is room for many ideals. Hold fast to the truth that appeals to you, for it is the truth. Never doubt that (Loc 1623, Kindle edition). "

Other books state, we are divided according to our development or level of progression. We are drawn by the law of attraction to those who are like us. We join others of like-mind with similar ideas, intentions, desires, and development. Like attracts like and souls of like affinity gravitate together. These are kindred souls, and souls of similar disposition and level of attainment remain together. We can continue with those who love us and are mentally akin. Raymond, Sir Oliver Lodge's son, in communications with him, states that like gravitates to like, that those who have antipathy part ways, and those in affinity remain together.

There are multiple planes based upon development and souls are not omniscient. They do not know everything. They only know what is in the realm of their environment and experience. They cannot venture to a higher plane unless invited or requested. They have no idea of what occurs on the higher planes and do not have the same knowledge as those who are far more developed.

Shanna Spalding St. Clair channels in *"Karma I and II"*, "There are limitations of knowledge at each level correlating with our stage of spiritual progression (23, 61)." We are only given the knowledge that we are capable of comprehending at our particular level of development.

Frederick Sculthorpe, in his book, *"Excursions to the Spirit World,"* states that those who are more developed come to visit the less developed planes to impart thoughts, feelings, and awareness of spiritual truth and wisdom. They are directly imbued with understanding from the more developed intelligences.

Some of those from more energized experience levels serve as guides to those who are less developed. The lives of those on earth can also be observed by those in the afterlife for teaching purposes. We all serve as teachers to one another. Gretchen Vogel states that we all are involved in a complex dance , assisting and edifying one another, and contributing to our personal evolution.

I had a relative who, while he was living, had a Christian background and belief system, and did not believe communicating with the dead was something that we should seek.

Since he has passed, he has communicated many details of his life, corroborating his identity, and states that the afterlife is even better than we imagined. One interesting episode that occurred while he was alive was a dream he had shortly after the passing of a good friend. There was a friend he had known for years with whom he remained in contact. This friend had done some negative things to others in his lifetime. He came to my relative in a dream and when my relative awakened, he was crying and said, "My friend told me he's not in a good place but he said right over there is a little better. I'll be able to get over there in a while ." My relative was not kidding. He was shaken by the dream and felt empathy for his friend, who was not able to communicate with him before he died as he had had a severe stroke.

This incident provided evidence for me that we gravitate to different levels of development in the afterlife based upon our actions and choices in this life. It is like a centrifuge- like seeks like, and each attracts his own based upon affinity. Those who are less developed, or have made more negative choices in their lifetime, do not earn or attain the same level as those whose actions and choices were more positive. We are all in constant development, and as we graduate from school in this lifetime, so we graduate from level to level in the afterlife as we progress and learn.

Shanna Spalding St Clair's book, "*Karma I and II*", refers to a hierarchy of development called the 7x7, with 7 major levels, each level containing 7 sub-levels. "We progress through the hierarchy of the 7x7, a hierarchical strata consisting of 7 levels, each with 7 sub-levels on our spiritual voyage through the reflection of the Oneness. We progress with forward movement. The 7x7 is the equivalent of ranking by progression or spiritual status (16, 20, 59)."

My friend, Laurie, a superb channeling medium, describes the advanced levels that higher dimensional beings inhabit. Some have never incarnated on the earth plane and some have. They describe themselves as energy. Karma II states that even ascended beings continue to have form until they reunite with Source (17, 63-64). They describe themselves as many souls who maintain individual consciousness but are part of a whole like the molecules within a cloud or the drops of water in the sea. Just as we on earth have limited conception of the nature of the afterlife, those on a particular level of the afterlife are not aware of what things are like several levels above them.

My guide states,

"There are gradations of development. We go with others with whom we have a vibrational affinity. We are together with those with whom we have a common bond. The truest bond of love pulls us together. There are different vibrational levels, and those are the levels we gravitate to based upon our development.

We can move up to a higher level of development when we are ready for it.

They are dimensions of vibration and can co-exist spatially but are yet separate from each other. When a soul ascends, it has transitioned to a different area of consciousness. There is separation between levels but they are sometimes breached for purposes of higher learning. Individual souls can visit other distinct planes of spiritual development, but cannot stay there unless they have reached that level of spiritual attainment. A vibrational assignation delineates a level, not necessarily a name."

Referring to souls who have reached a certain level of attainment in the afterlife and are now experiencing an earth incarnation, Shanna Spalding St. Clair, in "*Karma and I and II*", explains, "In what is referred to as the upper third level density, the incarnate initiates the desire for an inner search and the soul goes outside of itself to perform service for others. The connection with Spirit begins, with Spirit influence, assistance, and confirmations. In the fourth stage, humanitarian efforts are demonstrated. There is a search for self awareness and the encouragement of others to do the same. Meditation is employed. Only those who are ready for a certain understanding will receive it (77)."

Laurie's guides channel as follows, "In the advanced levels, higher dimensional beings or energies exist without bodies. Some have never incarnated and some have. There is no sexuality or gender. They do have form. Some have humanoid bodies and do have a male or female appearance. The many souls are a part of a whole, like the molecules within a cloud or the atoms in the sea. Those on a particular level cannot see several levels up."

A teacher from an advanced level channels through me,

"We have a stronger spiritual foundation. We are very much oriented toward helping other souls progress. We have bodies but not the kind you're familiar with. We have a visible component that we can bring forth into form. We have work that is involved in teaching and uplifting. We are all beings who have had a long spiritual track record. Some of us have been human and others not. If we wish, we can present ourselves in a humanoid form. I have an identity similar to what I had before, only more enlightened. We are more consciously connected with Source. We have learned what we needed to as humans, and now are pupils of the cosmic law. Higher principles, greater service, holier ethos, these are our pursuits. We are more involved in the realm of Godly wisdom than human endeavor. We are more concerned with the understanding and practice of spiritual values and ideals, manifested in action. "

Seven

# Reality

In one book a spirit said, contrary to what people ordinarily think, the spirit world is the real world, the permanent reality, and the physical world we inhabit, and regard as the real world compared with the intangible ethereal world of spirit, is just an illusion.

Although the physical world is real in the sense that objects and people exist and we can affect our environment, interact with it, and have real experiences, as well as see predictable cause and effect and natural laws, perhaps the physical world is an illusion in the sense that it is only a temporary portion of our experience as souls. It is not permanent, but only a fabricated, contrived temporary environment set up for us to learn lessons, a school so to speak, where we plan and set up situations for ourselves to learn, develop, progress, and grow.

Like a picture, it is real, but only a representation. In like manner, the physical body is the temporary house or clothing for the real person, the eternal soul. We pull off that clothing when we die. We move from our temporary journey or vacation on earth to our permanent home.

Reality is the lasting essence of who we are as souls, as individual consciousness. We and the world we inhabit are always changing. Reality is not static, it is fluid. It is always in flux. We all have some very deep essence that is us, that makes us eternal . We have an environment we interact with and inhabit. Existence is eternal, but the particulars, the situations change. They are fluid, dynamic. We always exist and we are always changing. The very spirit of us, the very core of us remains. As energy is not destroyed but changes form, so do we. The permanent reality is the lasting existence of our soul, in its change and development.

The reality we know is not fixed, but malleable, a temporary reality set up to learn lessons, real, but not permanent. The situations are planned to learn from, contrived or fabricated and as a picture is real, not the real person, but rather a representation. The reality we experience is like a play written by us, from which we learn lessons and grow.

My guide gave me an image in a dream that elucidates this. I was dreaming about an actress and seeing many interesting scenes from her life. I grew absorbed in the unfolding story and couldn't wait to see what happened next. Finally a point in the story came where she had to make the choice to go to a distant, unfamiliar land, or stay where she was, where she was comfortable. At that point the camera zoomed out and I saw a wide expanse of beautiful, blue ocean, looking down as if I were above, and I heard the words very distinctly, "The choice is yours."

I was shocked, but immediately understood that this scene was a metaphor for my life, that I was the actress acting in a play I had planned and designed, feeling the consequences of the choices I made and the situations I designed, exercising free will against a backdrop of planned events and relationships.

Souls exist. The experiences we have and the events we live through exist. Natural and Universal laws and principles exist. Reality is an illusion in the sense that our objective reality is not fixed or set. It changes from moment to moment, and can be shaped or altered by our will, thoughts, actions, and intentions. What was reality in one moment may not be reality in the next moment. Our individual reality is also colored by our perceptions.

A priest I once knew, named Dr. Fehring, said, "Objective reality is the common agreement of all subjective minds."

This physical world is an illusion to those in the afterlife because it is temporary, not a permanent reality for us. It is like a school for souls to learn lessons. All of what we perceive is limited by our senses- dogs' hearing and instruments prove that there is much more than we can hear, see, or sense. Even a table that appears solid to us is a collection of molecules and atoms that have space between them. So what we call reality on this physical plane is not the eternal true reality recognized by those in the afterlife.

Eight

# Right and Wrong

A spirit channeling in one of the books I read made the comment that there is no right or wrong. Yet, in the same book, it was also stated that the earth is a school and we are learning lessons. A lesson of itself implies that there is something to learn, a right or wrong answer. There must be something to learn, or there would be no need for a lesson.

My guide has told me that he is progressing on the other side. Progression implies something to progress to, some change for the better, some advancement, improvement, or working toward perfection.

If there were no principles, no morals, no right or wrong in our behavior and interactions, we would live in anarchy. We could harm one another, steal, rob, cheat, lie, and murder one another without repercussions. If you were the victim of these acts, would you agree that there is no such thing as right or wrong?

Perhaps the spirit meant that in terms of the lessons we devise for ourselves, there is no right or wrong lesson that we can learn from. We are here to experience all manner of right and wrong, pain, injustice, pleasure, and happiness. When we are the recipient of the actions, deeds, speech, and behavior of others, we decide for ourselves what is good and bad. We also learn about our behavior in terms of how it affects others.

There are many issues and answers that are not black and white, but are in shades of gray. Some things may be acceptable to or correct for one person but not for another.

But if there is a universal law, and I personally believe there is, I believe it would be to treat others with compassion and love, not to deliberately harm others. This would be encompassed in the golden rule, "Do unto others as you would have them do unto you."

One book I read stated that people who choose to do harm to others, what we commonly regard as wrong, have not sufficiently developed their personalities. Personality is the quality through which we choose to do right or wrong. The character is not altogether changed in the spirit world, but is improved and the rough edges are rounded off.

We learn to be understanding, sympathetic, helpful, and compassionate. That book states that we should seek an open mind, which will help us to see and realize the truth. It will be given to us, as well as the courage to act in the truth. Our actions can be constructive or destructive, and we are learning to choose the right and good, to let these materialize in our lives and character. We are encouraged to let the greater power of spirit shine through and infuse our physical lives, refining and beautifying them.

Charlotte Dresser, in her book, *"Life Here and Hereafter"*, says "There is a normal life here. We have high Ideals and live up to them (Loc 1651, Kindle edition)."

My guide says that every positive change you make in someone else's life is a gift both to you and to them. It is a ripple effect. All the ways you affect and change others are perpetuated by them and so passed on.

No one need be afraid to cross over. We all do wrong in our lives. If we were perfect, we wouldn't need to be here.

The only thing you need to do is desire to change for the better. Source or God will help you to do it lovingly. You will have the beautiful things you desire, the true fulfillment, happiness, and peace. Material things alone will never give this to you. Look at the suicides, divorces, murders, and unhappiness among those who had them. You must not seek to harm others. Forgive the wrongs others have committed against you in the hope that others will forgive you for the wrongs you have done.

Only wish or choose to do better, to become better, to think better and to act better and you will. That is all God or Source asks of you. Desire to change, be willing to change, and God or source will help you change.

Nine

# Earth Lessons

We come back to earth to learn lessons. If we were perfect and didn't need the lesson we wouldn't need to come back to learn it. In her book, "*Choices in the Afterlife*", Gretchen Vogel states, "Death is not the ticket to enlightenment, enlightenment happens in life if it is to happen at all. Learning to be a good human by making mistakes is different from a life dedicated to destructive acts and evil (28, 150). "

In his channeled message, Frederick WH Myers says that man reincarnates to learn lessons necessary for the soul's growth, man is put into the physical world to develop the spiritual.

If there is a lesson, there is an implication that there is an understanding, a recognition, an answer, or something to be learned. Progress implies that there is a place to progress toward and grow to, or something to achieve.

Some of the most painful lessons in life are the ones we learn the most from. We will not have undergone this pain in vain. We have chosen to learn from the situations we are in. The insights we have and the knowledge we gain change us and refine us and we become the best we can be through trial and tribulation.

In *"Karma I and II"*, the message is given, "We must hold deep within our hearts a warm gratitude for having the privilege of our present life in body and for being given the opportunities for growth no matter how painful they may be. We must be grateful for the chance to rise above obstacles and to learn from them and to incorporate this learning into the progress of our soul (70). "

These lessons develop character. We learn to conquer and control our own weaknesses. One book states that we should not lose the golden opportunity of improving our selves and benefiting others. The soul is described as a rough diamond with its beauty concealed until it is cut and polished. We must learn of wrong in order to master it. One saying I particularly like from *"Claude's Second Book"* is this, "In seeking the spirits of those they loved, many have found their own souls (97)."

My guide states,

"Don't ever stop or recede. Move forward. Learn and grow. We all have problems, but learning to solve them or overcome them gives us the accomplishment of building our own character.

Each of us planned our current life with certain lessons in mind needed for spiritual growth. Major relationships and events were planned in conjunction with other members of our soul group or family to mutually teach one another lessons. We have the free will to react to these planned situations as we choose and may or may not learn the lessons we intended to learn."

In Toni Winninger's book, *"Life Lessons, Our Purpose"*, the spirits channel, how do we identify what our life's lesson is? They state that we can determine what our main lesson is by thinking of what absorbs most of our thoughts, concerns, and fears. Whatever preoccupies our mind most is likely to be an important lesson. How do we know when we have successfully accomplished that lesson? They state that when our major overriding preoccupation and concern no longer troubles us and is no longer a major part of our thoughts, we have dealt with that lesson, and can move on to other lessons or pursuits, such as devotion to helping others.

Ten

# Progression in the Afterlife

My guide states,

"We are always the same spirit, always ourselves, growing and learning along the way, no matter how many different bodies we inhabit. You've always been yourself throughout constant changes, physically, mentally, and emotionally, the sum total of everything you've experienced so far, becoming wiser through experience. We must learn to overcome challenges, negativity, and despair. The success of our souls isn't measured by the obstacles we face, but by how we handle them when they come along.

My feeling is that we have more to learn always. I'm learning here now. We call it progression. I don't have the same feelings I had before because I learned from some things that I didn't do well. I am much more philosophical and able to realize things that I didn't on earth. I felt my life was designed to give me some understanding about my own character. I am able to take that new knowledge and reinvent parts of myself. I will not do things the way I did them before. I can make more choices that are positive. I have always been a person who wanted to do right but am now more aware of the consequences of my choices. I feel like I've made progress. I have tried to make myself more sensitive to others' feelings. Because I've been able to do that I am now a more kind, caring person. I never felt that I wasn't, but I'm now more aware of my actions and their effects.

We weigh our choices by the golden rule. We come to conclusions as to what course of action or choice would result in the greatest good for the greatest number of people. We discuss alternatives, we contemplate results of possible actions. We feel the impact of our choices from the viewpoint of others and on ourselves and gain wisdom in making choices that are of benefit to and produce greater happiness and positive outcome for all concerned.

When we cross over we find out why we came to earth, what our plan was. We recognize why we chose this incarnation, we find out what we were supposed to learn, what our planned lessons were, what we did, and didn't learn. We see a purpose. Then we understand what our choices and consequences were and what other choices we had, what we could have done. We also have input from guides and spiritual advisors. We can see the effects of what we did on others, and the effects of others' actions and words on us. We decide what we accomplished or learned and what we didn't. We have to decide for ourselves what the best course of action would have been in difficult situations. We are not given an absolute right and wrong but principles that dictate the relative impact of our choices to ourselves and others, enabling us to weigh the liabilities and benefits and come to decisions about the optimum choices we could have made.

We all are teachers to one another, but we have teachers on the other side who are specialists in their discipline and we continue to learn. We do have buildings where people go to congregate and to learn. No one is going to perish. We all live forever. We will all have a chance to better ourselves. We all have the opportunity to learn. We all try to improve our position. We are not able to see everything while we are on the earth. We only see a small amount of the afterlife. We each have an obligation to help ourselves and others. We are all on paths of our own choosing."

Some books I have read channel spirits saying there is no right or wrong. Then what is progress for? What are lessons for? Those on the other side state that they don't judge us. Perhaps this means since we are on earth to learn lessons and undergo situations of abuse, pain, and suffering in order to learn lessons, those in the afterlife don't judge us because these situations are set up to learn and grow.

They say we judge ourselves in the afterlife and undergo a life review wherein we see everything we did from the point of view of others and feel the pain we caused others, ourselves. But the idea that we learn lessons implies that there is something to be learned, a conclusion to be drawn, a right or wrong to realize. The fact that we are told there is a life review indicates there is a point in our lives and something to be understood. The fact that we are told we reincarnate and come back again if we fail to learn a lesson until we learn it and that we continue to progress and learn lessons on the other side would imply there is something to progress toward, a goal.

The words progress and lesson in themselves suggest there is a change, evolution, or modification of our thought, intention, action, or behavior that is desirable and correct. Therefore, I think there is an objective even if it is not black or white, a goal, even if it is in shades of gray. That is, I think we are to learn to treat others with kindness and compassion, to learn to handle bad situations lovingly as much as possible, and to act according to the golden rule, to do unto others as we would have done unto ourselves.

In "*Spirit World and Spirit Life,*" Charlotte Dresser channels, "That is the secret of if all- the upward climb (Loc 2101, Kindle edition)..." Each goes to his own place. That is where his congeniality is expressed;-to those of his own thought and purpose (Loc 2133, 2581, Kindle edition)."

In Anthony Borgia's book, "*Life in the World Unseen,*" he channels, "We gravitate to those of our own kind (Loc 2314, Kindle edition)."

Frederick Sculthorpe, in his book, "*Excursions to the Afterlife,*" states, "God's laws are absolutely fair. Who can complain when one's own self is both judge and jury (48)?"

"*Claude's Second Book*" (78) refers to the soul as a "rough diamond," being polished and shaped into something beautiful.

Shanna Spalding St. Clair, in "*Karma I and II,*" channels, "Healing is a form of teaching. Both healing and teaching result in learning and progression. These are inseparable causes and effects (295)." It is important to understand that the concept of teaching by example does not only utilize such life experiences as those upon your plane judge as positive. So, negative or evil experiences are also instances of this sort of teaching for they provide opportunities for obstacles to be met with positive solutions (103)." "Service to another is but an exercise in co-creation with the One Source. Service is an elevated form of learning within the soul's evolution. The earth plane incarnative experience maximizes the opportunity for service to other souls (94)."

My guide states,

> "We do feel there is a right and wrong originating from Source. We all vary in our concepts of right and wrong depending on what culture we came from and what our personal opinions are. In the afterlife we realize that we have no right to harm others. We also have a right to protect ourselves from harm. We choose in the afterlife to live in harmony with others with the freedom to live unharmed by others and harming no other. We live in an environment of love and helpful coexistence.
>
> We realize we should create a mutual harmonious coexistence with respect and concern for others and for ourselves without the negatives of hatred, fear, violence, duplicity, anger, deception, lies, theft, selfishness, and intent to harm. We seek to help and live in peace. We seek to act in, give, and receive altruistic love."

Gretchen Vogel states that on the other side we review our choices and their consequences. We identify regrets. We obtain a sense of closure and can explore the "what if's" of our former life. We forgive ourselves and others. We learn which choices lead to happiness and healing. We review what our lessons were and determine what we would have done if we had to do it over with the objective of learning to make better decisions and choices in a situation or relationship. We then incorporate this learning into our future choices and behavior. This contributes to the ever ascending scale of evolution.

We can progress both in our earthly incarnation as well as in the afterlife, but earth progressions proceed more quickly because of the difficulties and negative conditions we encounter on earth.

Eleven

# Fate and Free Will

If we undergo circumstances in life that were supposed to happen to us, are our lives governed by fate or free will?

My guide says,

"There is no such thing as fate. There are chosen circumstances we are likely to encounter that help us to learn the lessons we wanted or needed to learn. We create our own future with our desires, choices, actions, and behavior. Our thoughts ordain our ultimate course and pathway.

We plan our lives on the other side, our time of birth, families, major relationships, careers, and major life's obstacles . These things are a matter of our choice before coming to earth. When we encounter these situations on earth, we always have the power to change the life path we selected for ourselves earlier. Most of the time we are guided to adhere to the path we planned. But we are always free to alter things during an incarnation if we so choose.

However, we do have a free will, and react to those major planned situations with our free will choices. We also are able to make additional plans for our lives while we are on earth.

So life consists of a set of pre-planned choices resulting in our major life events, our free will reaction to those events, and our ability to change our preset path if we desire. In fact, we still retain free will after we pass. We can stay near the earth if we have desire or unfinished business. We can decide whether or not to reincarnate. In the negative earth environment where we encounter difficult circumstances, pain, and trouble, we are able to progress more quickly then we could in the more benign environment on the other side. We still choose our occupations, interests, and pursued relationships on the other side. We may work toward progressing to the next vibrational level very assiduously or remain on one level where we are comfortable for a long time. We also will have the choice to ascend back to Source, but this occurs or begins when we are ready. All of these things remain within the scope of our free will. Even the choice to remain in lower or more negative states of understanding is ours."

We truly are the masters of our fate, the captains of our soul, as the poem by William Ernest Henley states.

Twelve

# Choices in the Afterlife

In the afterlife, thought creates all things. In spirit, we create our own reality. Per the medium, Laurie, we are creating our future with our thoughts. She states, "You and your partner are co-creating together. When two souls love each other and have chosen to be together, they co-create their future lives together with their thoughts and intentions. You have to find your own truth." We are making our own lives and happiness. In the larger sense, "The past makes the future and you are the director". One of the other mediums in the Bahamas said, "There are many things that we create with our thoughts, which produce material results and manifest as objects."

Frederick WH Myers channeled, "In this invisible world there is infinite variety of conditions. I can only speak of what I know. When we hold on to dogma or limited vision, consciousness of the greater reality is held from us. We are light inhabiting an image, etherealized form. We become an individualized part of the whole with no need for expression in form. The unreality of the material world lies in the fact that while we are in form we only see a part of the picture. "

Other writers have indicated that what we experience in the afterlife depends to an extent on what we are like, what we seek, what we are eligible for based upon our character. You will find those you really love.

"The dead can only describe what they have personally experienced. When we are in earthly form we only see a part of the picture. There lies the unreality of the material world. In this invisible world there is infinite variety of conditions. I can only speak of what I know. "

Another author states, "What we experience in the afterlife depends to an extent on what we are like, what we seek, and what we are eligible for based upon our level of development. Our experience is individual- based upon our own character. It can be similar to our earth experience or vastly different. It is originator dependent. Those who have the greatest intense bond or affinity will be together. The dead can only describe the actual experience of things about them. You will find those you really love. "

My guide states,

"I can express my knowledge from the vantage point I see. Just as on earth we have different understandings of truth and interpret reality differently based on our unique perspective, viewpoint, or level of development, so we in the spiritual world have different conclusions, ways of apprehending based upon our own individual interpretations. We are not instantly omniscient or perfect. We continue to learn and grow at different levels, as upon the earth. Knowledge is greater, but opinions remain.

We have a great diversity of choices on the other side. We can choose the kind of environment we inhabit and the souls we interact with. We have choices in our recreation and our leisure. We do have choices in our work and we are freer in choices then we were on the earth. We are not required to stay with a soul with whom we are not compatible due to a marriage bond. We do not have to do a job we don't like to earn a living. We don't have to maintain houses or inhabit a physical body with aging and pain. We don't have crime, theft, or criminal activity. We cannot lie or cheat. Our true natures are revealed. We have similar types of activity and interests except with the negative aspects of the earthly plane absent.

There are many people who have different ideas regarding the afterlife and they can all see what they want to see. We create our reality so we can make it objective. We originate our own lifestyle and surroundings. The imaginings we create become reality. For those of us who failed to experience our dreams while on earth, we can complete the things that we didn't complete on the earth."

Gretchen Vogel, in her book, *"Choices in the Afterlife,"* states, "Everything we can imagine after death is possible to experience to some extent, if only within our own mental reality (73, 145) ".

Regarding social relationships, we can choose to be alone but don't have to. We remain in an environment with those we love. We can have an even deeper relationship with greater intimacy then we did with someone we loved on earth. We can have circumstances similar to those on earth such as a home, if we choose. We do not need to express a gender or play a particular role. We can experience the type and depth of relationship we prefer.

Gretchen Vogel indicates, "Although we are energy, we can put back on bodily form of a prior life if we wish (20, 58, 64, 148)."

Thirteen

# Karma

The law of karma is not a law of retribution, but of action and reaction. We reap what we sow. If we don't get an education, getting a good job is more difficult. If we don't pay for health insurance, we will have more trouble obtaining medical care. We experience the consequences of our previous actions and choices.

I understand that the karmic cycle can be broken in relationships by mutual forgiveness and the cessation of negative actions and behavior. In *"Karma I and II"*, Shanna Spalding St. Clair explains, "Karma results from our choices and deeds and its purpose is to overcome the negative and choose the positive, avoid the wrong and embrace the right. Our path is our chosen set of circumstances and experiences in a given life that will allow us to learn a needed lesson, to change or improve our understanding, choices, and behavior. Our Karma depends on how we react to the experiences and conditions we endure. Our will allows us to create the experience and then to make the proper choice that allows us to grow from the experience. We create our own journey (76, 84). "

St. Clair, in *"Karma I and II,"* channels that as souls we each were broken off from Source with a God given intent.

Gretchen Vogel, in *"Choices in the Afterlife,"* states that we are here on earth to fulfill our God given intent (166).

Karma is the result of our actions. It makes sense to say that we have to live the consequences of our choices. We always have to feel what we have caused others. Without consequences there would be no learning. We don't have to relive all aspects of what we have done. If something is necessary for our progress or our learning, we may choose upon the advice of our guides and counselors, to live through that experience. We choose to do so not because we have to, but because we are encouraged to, and need to for our continual improvement.

We have Karma if we feel we need to experience something in order to grow. It is the natural outcome of our actions, the law of action and reaction, cause and effect. We are very strongly advised to complete certain learning experiences but we always have free will. We don't need to repeat all things. If we didn't finish a lesson we don't always need to complete it, but often we do. We can repeat it under different circumstances or in a different manner. If we achieve our karmic task in any given incarnation, we can expand beyond it and set additional goals with the assistance of our guides.

We can overcome the effects of our negative actions through mutual forgiveness and replacing negative with positive behavior. We overcome our past Karma and are changing it all the time by our ongoing actions, feelings, and choices. We can choose to overcome it. We need to learn lessons by being placed in situations and reacting to them. Karma is what helps us grow. As we lead better lives, we alter our Karma.

We aren't aware of all the reasons why things happen when we are alive. When we cross over, we see why we had to experience certain things and what we were supposed to learn from it. All of our actions, thoughts, and deeds have consequences. That is the way we learn. We understand that what we do has repercussions.

We are able to learn by personal experience why we should be more kind, more caring, and more loving. We don't see that until we experience our own deeds coming back to us. We often don't know how something feels until we feel it ourselves. We learn by experience and example. Through personal involvement we are able to grow. I had a personal experience in which I was taught a lesson by my guides. After the lesson concluded, I heard the words, "Now I know what that feels like. "It is certainly a lesson I will never forget.

In *"Karma I and II,"*, Shanna Spalding St. Clair channels an advanced soul group discussing Karma. "The negative earth environment provides a compressed karmic learning opportunity. We have a karmic task to perform when we come to earth (23, 26, 66, 93)." "We also have a karmic commitment to other souls who are on the path based on past interactions and contracts that we made in the afterlife. We must justify any incarnation in the physical from the viewpoint of its helping our progression as well as that of the other souls we interact with (19, 43, 67)." "We incarnate for karmic interaction resulting in the most advantageous opportunities to advance the mutual progression and karmic task of the group of light beings. When we cross over we will perceive the total interactive purposes (25, 38, 54, 65)." "We maintain form that permits us to be perceived by other light beings that can create in a similar pattern. Thus, we co- create and reaffirm our mutual existence and assist each other's forward movement. This is how we learn our most valuable lessons. Our goal in incarnation is enlightened choice (17, 63-64)."

As *"Karma I and II,"* explains, we enter the physical environment to experience trial and error situations, problematic situations that cause affronts to us physically emotionally and mentally. Certain karmic areas cannot be advanced by less traumatic or confrontational experiences. Evil is permitted to occur as it provides opportunities for obstacles to be met with positive solutions. We should be grateful even for tragedy if it provides the opportunity to learn. All experience should prod us to positive thought and action.

In a television show called The Unexplained, the comment was made, "There is karmic justice. It had to unfold exactly in the way it did."

If we recognize that we script our lives on the other side and act out roles with contracts with other souls to place ourselves in situations to learn lessons we need to learn or teach others the lessons they need to learn, it makes sense that we should be able to forgive them in the afterlife, especially if we planned to undergo a situation in order to learn from it. Also, if we deliberately harmed another soul in a previous lifetime and we now have to undergo that harm ourselves in order to learn from it, it also makes sense that we should be able to forgive that soul.

We must learn what things feel like both so that we can understand behavior and so that we do not desire to harm other souls. It has been explained that in the life review we experience after our transition to the spirit realm we experience the pain we caused others as they experience the pain they caused us.

In "*Karma I and II,*" Shanna Spalding St. Clair states , "You cannot force another soul to have spiritual fulfillment. You can only facilitate their attaining it themselves (79, 91-92)."

Fourteen
# Reincarnation

We are all able to reincarnate if we wish. We don't have to. We can. We often reincarnate because we wish to progress as quickly as possible. Many souls participate in soul groups or soul families on the other side. These are groups of souls that often reincarnate together for the purpose of learning and often have had many reincarnations together. Any soul has the choice of reincarnating separately if it wishes to. Most souls prefer to reincarnate with a soul group.

In the spirit realm, reincarnation is considered a misnomer. In actuality, souls undergo a series of successive or consecutive incarnations, since the successive levels in the afterlife are considered incarnations as well, since souls maintain form until they reunite with Source.

As Shanna Spalding St. Clair indicates in her book "*Karma I and II*," "Incarnation occurs as a result of the need for Karmic progression. We transmute the outward manifestation of our existence into physical form. We choose a particular incarnation so that lessons can be acquired (81, 223). In order to justify a particular incarnation, all incarnating souls must benefit from that incarnation (35, 36, 67). When the will is relinquished, death follows (85). "

The channeling continues, "The soul form energy complex is always in the pure definition of incarnation, within a state of incarnation, until it is rejoined with the One Source from which it came (108)."

The channeled messages of F. W. H. Myers indicate that man reincarnates to learn lessons necessary for his soul' s growth. Man is put into the physical world to develop the spiritual.

Other authors have channeled spirits indicating that we are aware that there are other places in the universe that are habitats of life. There are other life forms. Some are what we know of as physical and some are not. All are life but some cannot be seen by others because of our vibrational and visual limitations. They are as much life as we in the physical are. They are of another spectrum/vibrational/dimensional form of life. They are not the same as we are, but as real as we are, just not perceived by us.

We are able to access our past lives. We are aware of them, but not in great detail. We are able to look into them and access the details if we wish.

We didn't create ourselves. Vanity is foolish pride. Any abilities or talents we have we were born with. We did not create them or give them to ourselves. We only develop or use them. Those who do things should do them for the joy of the act itself, not for the adulation of others. We should feel gratification in the accomplishment, not from the admiration of others, which is foolish, and can come and go.

A kind deed, a kind act, a loving or compassionate gesture is worth far more than a magnificent creation. Magnificent creations can bring joy and pleasure and have worth, but not as much worth as an unselfish deed or charitable kindness performed from the heart. Such are the most marvelous creations, that affect others lives for the good, that are positive and ripple through eternity, bettering the lives of others, so much finer then an artistic design, song, or entertainment .

Fifteen
# World of Illusion

The world of illusion, sometimes called the world of conceptual reality, is considered a stage of the afterlife in which we can create our own idealized world with like-minded souls. It is an idealized world, the creation of our imagination, and the fulfillment of our dreams. It has been called an idealized or perfected earth. William Buhlman, who is the author of multiple books on astral projection, in a lecture at the Monroe Institute, referred to it as a consensus reality created by group thought of a number of souls who are projecting their idea of Heaven. Gretchen Vogel, in "*Choices in the Afterlife*", states that spirits can create a temporary reality with their belief system. As it is temporary, it is considered an illusion, not a permanent reality. We can continue our earthly experiences on the plane of illusion. She describes one spirit as saying I can eat and eat and don't gain an ounce.

Charlotte Dresser, in her book "*Spirit Life and Spirit World*", written through automatic writing, was told that if you miss a picnic, you can have one. It will all be yours, picnic and all. If we want something we loved or didn't have in life, we can have it (Loc 1640, Kindle edition). "Don't worry! You will find the counterpart of every pure joy here. All the joys you have there will only be intensified here (Loc 1615, Kindle edition)."

John Scott, in his book, *"From One Ghost to Another"*, says man on the other side still imagines he must satisfy his hunger and seek wealth, love, or ease in one accustomed way or another. They can do what they like. They try to satisfy their desires, and surprised, believe they are enjoying the real thing they remember. They repeat past experiences with their new increased powers and faculties (32-33).

Raymond, the son of Sir Oliver Lodge, communicating through automatic writing in the book *"Raymond, or Life and Death"*, states, " Spirits can also come over with earthly desires (198)." They must wean newcomers from earthly desires such as eating and drinking. They may partake of earthly desires until weaned.

FWH Myers channels through automatic writing, all of the activities of their previous life can be re-enacted if such is their will. They can adapt the memory world to their taste, including the old pleasures, without difficulty, satisfying their desires. These activities will seem real to them. They can gratify sexual desire, created by memories and imagination. They can live within the fantasy created by their strongest desires on earth.

You can co-create a consensus reality. You can shape your surroundings to your vision. You can create your own version of the appearances you knew on earth. Your emotional desires and your higher mind manufacture these. It is called the illusion world and is formed by the concentrated thought of men.

In this world we can fulfill all of the things we didn't fulfill on earth. Laurie, a physical and mental medium, channels, "Although desires we have on earth drop away as we progress, this is not always necessarily true. Certain desires important to an individual may persist for a longer or shorter period of time, especially if they were particularly important to that person or if they represented a deep psychological need, or were deeply desired but not fulfilled on the earth plane. These desires, if not harmful to others, can be fulfilled even if by creating an illusionary experience which will seem real to the participant. "

My guide states,

> "We do not usually eat, drink, or have sex, because we lose the biological drive for these activities when we lose the physical body. We can, however, reproduce a situation similar to the act of eating or sex if we have a strong psychological desire to do so. It is called an illusion because it is temporary, as the earth life is, but feels real to those creating and experiencing it. We can have deep seated emotional desires though we no longer have physical needs or compulsions."

Frederick WH Myers channels, in the world of memory or illusion man can live within the fantasy created by his strongest desires on earth, created by memories and imagination.

Sixteen
# Spirit Body

I and many others who have lost loved ones ask the question what do spirits look like? What does my loved one look like in the afterlife? Can we ever hug and kiss again? In her book, *"Karma I and II"*, Shanna Spalding St. Clair channels that energy achieves form. We have form until we reunite with God. We are consciousness, forms of light, which have separate existence . We can choose to ascend to Source but not reunite, and still maintain a separate form. She refers to us as a soul form energy complex consisting of multiple bodies of varying density, including the human or personality body, the astral, mental, and etheric bodies. We also have an oversoul, which contains the cosmic soul print or master plan of our identity (54).

A discarnate being does not mean that entity has no substance or form but that it does not have a physical body as we know it. We have control of our appearance. We have a higher vibrational body. Our bodies or substance becomes more rarefied as we ascend in plane or dimension.

Charlotte Dresser, channeling information about Spirit appearance, states that Spirit is substantial, material, more real than the physical world. "You seem to think there is no substantiality to spirit, while we know it's the only substantiality (Loc 1056, Kindle edition)." "Spirit is higher in the scale of existence than matter; therefore, we are more real than we were in our material forms (Loc 1401, Kindle edition)."

When asked if we maintain a form similar to our earthly appearance, the medium, Laurie, channels, "We can go between energetic form and body. Most keep a human type of form on the lower levels. We are known by vibration, but usually keep a name for a while. We can change to our energetic form, which is more efficient, when we travel. Conditions at the lower planes are more earth-like. We can assume a more physical type of body if we wish. Usually this is done for purposes of comfort or contact with loved ones and for purposes of touch, speech, and other things that are reminiscent of our earthly lives. We tend to have humanoid -type bodies on the first three or four planes or levels ".

In " *Claude's Second Book*", he said," We have solid bodies and they are controlled by our thoughts. In our conditions our bodies are quite as solid as yours, but in as far as they are matter, they are completely under the control of mind (19)."

My guide states,

"We are able to have a body similar to that we had on the earth if we wish to hug or kiss. Although our normal mode of communication is telepathy or clairvoyance, we are able to speak or use words if we wish. We normally have a finer body, but can have a body equivalent to the earthly body if we wish."

Charlotte Dresser, in her book, " *Life Here and Hereafter*", channels this information. "The spirit body has sight, hearing, thought, and touch (Loc 795, Kindle edition)." "Although etheric in substance, we have the semblance of these in Spirit form. We can well assume the outline of the material form. We can change our appearance with our thought. We keep the old familiar form (Loc 808, Kindle edition)."

Gretchen Vogel indicates in her book, "*Choices in the Afterlife*, "We are creating our own experience and can change our age and appearance. Through the projection of the deceased's mind, we clothe ourselves with the memory of the prior body at whatever age is desired. We look solid. My memory body feels as real to me as yours does to you. I take walks. I curl up in my favorite chair at home (13). Those who have crossed over state that although they are not needed, they can have houses if they wish."

My guide states,

> "We have choices. We are an electromagnetic energy field that can manifest as substance with form. I am not set or fixed as on the earth. We are able to choose how we look. I am an energy that manifests in different ways. I can look solid and appear as I did on the earth or take the form of a mist, a ball of light, or an orb. We choose how we want to look and can change our appearance with our thoughts. We are made from a more malleable spirit substance that we can change at will. If I choose to have a human form, I can look like I did in my most recent lifetime, a prior lifetime, or any other way I choose. Most prefer to look as they did on earth in their prime. If we choose to have a earth type body, we can speak, embrace, and look like we did on earth.

Our bodies, however, may look the same but are not the same internally. We do not have the internal organs or processes."

According to Frederick WH Meyers, you can control form, shape your own vehicle and surroundings according to your vision. According to William Buhlman, spirits co-create a consensus reality.

My guide states,

"We can sense vibrational signature and personality. We do not need to have a human type of body to tell who we are or to communicate, but these things are available to us if we desire. We see each other through the direct apprehension from mind to mind. We also hear each other that way. We don't need the intermediary sense organs. We see and hear directly through our own minds. We sense vibration that way also. We have Spirit senses that interpret the unique vibrations of others. We understand and sense them with our thoughts. We interpret their energy. We feel the essence, substance, and energy of another. Through this interpretation of vibration, we have vision, knowing, thought, and feeling. We live through our thoughts. We can appear solid to each other.

We can change our appearance at will. Those who choose to can look like they did on earth. We can also have a favorite human type form that we had previously in the afterlife. We can maintain the appearance we had in our recent incarnation if we like that appearance or to appear in a familiar form for a loved one we are greeting who has recently passed. Some wish to maintain an energetic form. We can interchange and adopt these forms at will."

Anthony Borgia's book, "*Life in the World Unseen*", refers to souls in the afterlife as possessing bodies or form, not physical bodies, but etheric bodies which are a replica of our old physical form. He also refers to structures and buildings in the afterlife. As the afterlife is so vast, and can be manifested differently according to the varying desires of groups of spirits, one soul's reality may not be another soul's reality. Also, there are multiple habitats, levels, and planes in the afterlife, just as there are multiple locations on earth. What may be true for one living in one locale may be entirely different for someone residing in another locale.

The channeled message continues, "We are able to see and hear and touch each other on our plane, and feel solid to each other (Loc 1973, Kindle edition)."

A message channeled through the medium, Laurie, states, "Most of the time souls have a designated sexuality. Generally, males are larger. There are choices. There's everything. If you want to be male or female you can be male or female. Other spirits are neither. You can go back and forth. You do have a set appearance on the other side that is not related to your incarnations. Souls have different looks and shapes. You can change your appearance, if you like, for something better. We remember more of our past lives here than you do. You can pick an incarnation you like to identify with if you want. Most of the time people find something they are comfortable with and stick with it."

My guide indicates,

"Names are not needed on the other side. As you recognize someone you know by appearance, you recognize someone you know in the afterlife by energetic imprint or vibrational signature. Our energetic imprints are unique, like fingerprints or DNA. No two are identical. If we choose to energetically maintain a humanoid type of body, a subtle ethereal equivalent of our physical body, we can use names and even have nicknames for each other. Our energetic form is a changeable cloud- like focal accumulation of energy. We are a somewhat amorphous energy field but can change forms and shapes with thought and intention. We can take on bodies to interact in a more human manner. We often choose to look like we did in a recent incarnation so that those who are crossing over see us in a familiar form."

Seventeen

# Spirit Senses

I wondered, how do spirits see, hear, feel, and touch? Do spirits have the same sensory input that we have? My guide has told me that spirits communicate thoughts and feelings telepathically. There is mind to mind transfer of thoughts and images.

> "We don't need a language. We have instantaneous thought transmission. We exchange thoughts easily."

They directly feel and sense one another. Frederick WH Myers communicates, we practice clairvoyance and communicate through feeling. We can also speak as you do. When we first undergo the change that is called death, many of us desire to see each other and use words the way we used to, and many continue long in that state of mind.

We know one another more thoroughly than we ever could on earth. We can't hide our true personality. Our inner being is transparent and our true self is known to others. We cannot hide our true character or lie. Our inner qualities will shine through and our real character is apparent. We gravitate to the level of development appropriate to us and reside with kindred souls.

Gretchen Vogel states that the essential nature of the deceased does not change just because they don't have a physical body. The sensory memory body interprets information similar to the way in which the nervous system senses things, based upon memory of sensual experience. Sensation is based upon the memory of physical sensation-the memory of what this would have looked and felt like when they were in the body.

My guide states,

"Just as all sensations including sight and hearing are transmitted as waves/particles and received by a cellular mechanism causing chemical changes which generate a neural transmission received by the brain, in Spirit sight, sound, and hearing, the middleman is removed. While senses on earth are mediated through receptor cells with chemical changes and interpreted through electrical impulses in vibrations and waves, we now receive that vibration/electrical impulse directly. Since we are electromagnetic energy without the needed intermediary of sense organs, thoughts and sensations are transferred directly. The energetic vibrations corresponding to sight or hearing are perceived directly by the interpreting energy and cognizant consciousness. Just as we can see without eyes and hear without ears and speak without organs of speech by direct trans-mission and reception, we can feel all sensations of touch without direct stimulation of a nervous system. If we so desire, we can have bodies similar to the physical body in order to kiss, hug, and touch.

But we can convey a feeling, a thought, a visual impression or sensation through our minds directly to another mind. We can decode their vibration and their vibration registers with us in an impression. It impresses on our mind a picture, a thought, a concept, a vision, a feeling, or a sensation. We send and receive these impressions. That is how we communicate. We direct our energy to another and can receive their energy. We are able to translate it and convert it to a picture, an idea, a sense impression, or a concept."

A spirit channeling through Gretchen Vogel in her book, "*Choices in the Afterlife*, "explains it this way. Light from an object or scene was reflected in through my eyes, my optic nerves, to my brain. This activated a chemical reaction that told me what I was looking at. I will still get the same information from what I focus on, but the information comes directly into my mind instead of through my eyes. My mental perception is as accurate as if I was seeing it with my eyes. I hear things because of the vibration that sound makes. I can hear people talking clearly.  Hearing is the one that is most like it was when I was in the body. The sound is picked up all over my memory body (21-22). "

A message channeled through Charlotte Dresser indicates, "We have sensations analogous to the mortal ones in a spiritual sense (Loc 982, Kindle edition)."

Paranormal investigators  report being touched by spirits, having their hair pulled or being scratched. Spirits communicating through mediums can describe what a person's house looks like or talk about events that occurred after their decease. They continue to attend events that are important to loved ones left behind. They can describe what we are wearing or eating. They can move physical objects, turn faucets on and off, and communicate through flashlights and EMF meters. All of this data suggests that spirits continue to see people, objects, and places.

Lisa Williams, in her book, "*The Survival of the Soul* ", describes astrally projecting, and how when she was out of the body she could see places and people who could not see her. She also describes a visit to the afterlife in which she meets her soulmate and describes a humanoid appearance. Others who have had near death experiences describe meeting loved ones who have passed, who looked like they had before and felt solid. They were able to hug and kiss them.

A medium who works in the medical profession and I shall refer to as Karuna, channeled a group of souls who answered a question of mine. I asked, "Do we have Spirit senses on the other side that are the equivalent of our physical senses of seeing hearing and touch? If not, how are they different?" I was told, "There are Spirit senses but they are not equivalent. One does not need eyes to see or ears to hear. There are understandings and awarenesses that are far beyond these. There is no need to be concerned that one will miss those senses. Your senses are developed so that you can bring in information, experience, awareness, and understanding so that you can process thoughts. The senses are relay systems, an added series of steps required in the physical to experience your thoughts and emotions. The senses are a vehicle for our experience. We will have all experiences available to us that we previously had through the mediations of our physical senses. All of these are available to us in spirit. There is experience of those things that you find vital to your essence in order to develop and feel satisfaction. "

Eighteen

# Sex and Touch

Spirits are comprised of electromagnetic energy and normally take the form of a discrete concentrated energy field. They can appear as a luminous cloud of moving energy, a ball of light, or an orb. They can transform that energy into various forms at will, including the semblance of a human body, either similar to or different from the one they had in their last incarnation. They are not confined to a single, stable form, as on earth. "If we reside in a spirit body, which has form and substance, we can be seen by those inhabiting the same level of vibration." This energy is vibrating at a higher rate and is not normally seen on the earth plane. Occasionally, with enough energy, they can manifest on the physical plane.

They can create or assume various forms. Some communications such as those from Anthony Borgia, in *"Life in the World Unseen"*, indicate, "We are able to see and hear and touch each other on our plane and feel solid to each other as we did on earth. Each successive dimension or plane is of a higher and finer vibration, and although not appreciated or seen to those on a lower level, appears solid to those inhabiting that level (Loc 1973, Kindle edition). "

William Buhlman comments that on one astral excursion he encountered a relative who appeared as he did in the physical body when he was alive and was able to hug him. Many people in near death experiences have been able to see, touch, and hug previously deceased loved ones. People who have had paranormal encounters describe being touched, feeling the imprint of a hand or finger.

Toni Winninger channels Elvis Pressley in one of her books. He states that he can put on a more physical type of body which he uses when he is singing to and entertaining children who have recently crossed over.

My guide indicates,

"We can touch or feel each other when in the spirit body, but it isn't the same as earthly touch. It doesn't feel identical to skin. If we wish, we can use our energy to create and inhabit a body more similar to the one we had on earth. We can feel solid to each other. We can experience that hug or kiss if we want to. We can experience sexual passion and sexual union if we so desire. We can have sex in the afterlife. We create a temporary, illusionary reality for ourselves from our thoughts and it will feel real to us."

I have had several experiences with a loved one in spirit. In one instance I felt a soft touch on my arm that moved the skin and soft tissues. It felt real and unmistakable. In other instances I have felt his electromagnetic field. It is a soft, tingling sensation.

Bruce Moen, in his astral adventures, describes contact with a spirit energy field or body and the ability to feel that vibration as a sensation, to sense essence.

Craig Hamilton Parker states that, according to his communications, sex is relatively unimportant in the afterlife. As the physical drives are absent, sex is no longer a priority. However, for those who have a psychological or emotional need, the sex act can be simulated or performed. People can choose to maintain form resembling the human body with sexual organs if they desire.

Others, including Craig Hamilton parker, have described merging, a process in which souls superimpose, blend, and temporarily suffuse their energy bodies, joining them together. Each can mutually know and experience or feel the other's thoughts, ideas, emotions, and feelings, achieving a temporary union that is more intimate than the sexual union in the physical body.

The medium, Laurie, channels the information, "In the afterlife, we are able to create the illusion of having sex as we would have on earth and it will feel real to us." We create the temporary illusion with our thoughts. We can have a mutually shared union.

In "*Karma I and II*", the question is raised, "Is there the physical or emotional sensation of love when one is in spirit? Whatever awareness is necessary for the progression of a soul in spirit will be made available to that soul. In spirit, one creates one's own reality (35). "

Frederick WH Myers also channels that for those souls to whom sex is a deeply important psychological need, they can recreate that experience. It will be provided for them.

Charlotte Dresser, communicating in her book, "*Spirit World and Spirit Life*", channels the message, "We have sensations analogous to the mortal ones in a spiritual sense, although we don't gain them through the mortal organs. We have the spiritualized form of affection which is higher and finer. Thought expresses the emotion so you don't need touch, kiss, embrace, but we can have these if we wish. We can choose to have the sense of touch. Spirit can give sensation as perfectly as nerves. We can have intimate companionship. You will find the counterpart of every pure joy here. All the joys you have there will only be intensified here (Loc 982, 1615). "

Nineteen
# Merging

My guide comments,

"Merging is the temporary complete immersion, blending, and union of two souls into one. Each knows and feels the other's thoughts, feelings, emotions, and sensations with an exchange of energies more intimate then any we have known. It is an explosion of emotional bliss and rapture, an experience of total oneness, an ecstatic union more intense than the sexual experience of earth. When we merge we interpenetrate, mesh and superimpose our energy fields in a transcendent, ineffable euphoria."

Merging is usually performed by two souls with a very deep love for one another and desire for the ultimate closeness. Merging can be performed by any two deeply loving souls and is not an exclusive act, but is not typically a frivolous act.

Merging can be performed with different intentions and the nature of the experience is colored by those intentions. It can be performed by two souls who have once been mother and daughter or two souls who have been lovers. As most of us have had multiple lifetimes and related to each other in multiple capacities-for instance, two souls may have been a father and son in one lifetime, brother and sister in another, and husband and wife in yet a third-we have played many roles with each other. On the other side we have no set roles. Although we have the recall of having been a mother, a son, a sister, a wife, a husband, a grandparent, a friend, etc. to many others in many different lifetimes, we do not have one set type of relationship with another soul, but have experienced many. Also, as souls, we have no fixed gender, and have variously been male and female. After death, we are simply souls, relating to one another as we choose.

If we choose to maintain a particular type of relationship with another soul, or regard them as a parent, child, sibling, friend, or mate, we can. Therefore, the feelings accompanying merging, and the intention for the merging can be different for each pair of souls that merge.

There are souls who continue to remain couples, pairs, or mates on the other side. Although marriage is not needed, for there are no traditional roles of husband and wife, such as childrearing, homemaking, or providing and supporting, and there is no need to legally bind souls together who do not love one another for the sake of protection of children or fulfilling financial obligations to support a wife or husband, souls can make a spiritual commitment to one another. This is referred to as union. Two souls making such a commitment enact a vow or pledge to one another in the Akashic records to remain together throughout existence. Although there is no eternal irrevocably binding vow, a serious agreement of this nature is not entered into lightly.

Although merging is not an exclusive act, souls who have chosen to unite frequently choose to merge only with one another, not with others, reserving that intimacy exclusively for themselves.

My guide continues,

> "We can become closer than we ever did on earth with another soul because we have a clear understanding of their thoughts and feelings. We will literally feel as they do and know their thoughts, experiencing them as vividly as if they were our own. We each directly experience what the other experiences. We know without a doubt what someone else thinks and feels. There are no misunderstandings, lack of clarity, dissimulation, lies, or deception. We combine our energies. We blend our thoughts, feelings, and emotions as well as our substance, energy, or inner essence completely with that of another. Although we retain our identities, we transiently join as one soul. It is an epiphany of bliss and union that cannot be achieved on earth."

The feelings of consuming exhilaration, joy, love, oneness, completion, fulfillment, and entire union are shared simultaneously. It is an empathy more intense than any you can imagine. You have become one being in exultation, celebration, and joy.

My guide states,

> "We can come together, overlay, and blend our thoughts and feelings in a way that is more intimate and intense than the expressions of affection we had in the physical body, an ecstatic union of

feelings, thoughts, and sensations, an absolute oneness and union. We become completely immersed in one another as one being. We have different kinds of merging based on intention as we have different kinds of kisses and hugs on earth based upon intention. We can maintain the kind of romantic thoughts and passion we had in the body if we wish to have them. We do not have biological drives or needs, but we can have psychological desires. If we wish to, we can also create an equivalent to the earthly body to fulfill them. But we can engender the same feelings directly via merging that we would have attained by hugging and kissing on earth. This is another tangible means of communicating affection. Merging is not an indiscriminate act but is engaged in by two deeply loving, emotionally and spiritually bonded energies. It is a true act of love, but can also include romantic feelings if that is how the two souls feel about one another. It is the ultimate intimacy ."

The medium, Laurie, channels her guides, "Merging is done by two spirits that have a fulfilling, strong bond. It is a blending of two beings into one, so close we can't even conceive of it. There is a sexual quality or feel to it. You feel the other person's vibration and essence. Two become one. When you merge you will feel who he is and the love and respect he has for you as if it were in your own body. It feels like emotional rapture or bliss. A sexual act can be part of what it is if so chosen. Merging can be a sexual reaction if it pleases you. There is a component at times if it's agreed upon prior to the merge to connect with memories that simulate a sexual relationship. In that instance, there would be the sensation brought through in your body, not brought through in the same way, of the feel of an orgasm, a little bit of Heaven. That is one part of a sexual relationship you can experience in a different respect. Some here merge frequently."

Lisa Williams, in one of her classes, described merging in this way, "When you love someone so much you want them under your skin, that is what merging is like-energy attraction ".

The medium, Karuna, channeling an answer to my question about what merging is like, states, "We would say perhaps, not looking at things so much in comparison, but more so, what is it about life that creates its continuation? These aspects of continued life that bring forth opportunities to express love, higher and higher levels of understanding of the spiritual essence of the self and having relationships and understandings of others' experience, is very much a part of that and remains the same. We would say that as one becomes more aware and evolves in deeper understandings of the vibrational essence of life, we would say as that progresses one understands more deeply and expresses more deeply the joy of another and that togetherness becomes larger and larger and more expanded. So again we would say making comparisons to the way you experience the relationship with another is only one small aspect of that same experience. When not necessarily having the earth experience, you need to have a larger perspective when expressing a lighter vibrational form. How that manifests is not something that can be described by looking at a piece of paper with a picture or by stringing words together in a sentence. We would say that the best way to catch a glimpse of this experience would be to sit with yourself and remember deeply those experiences in your life in which you felt very connected to another soul, experiencing the joy in the manner that combines both of you, or perhaps many of you, in an expanded way, so that one love becomes greater. You still know that you are not all of the other soul, but the two souls or the many souls experience greater joy than one.

In summary I would say that it may make things easier to approach a question this way. Rather than from a comparative perspective, try to know your own energy through introspection. Let that awareness of your energy become so familiar to you that your own energy becomes a teaching tool for you to understand the greater spiritual perspective on all of those questions, such as, how does one communicate with another soul outside of the earth plane. "

Twenty

# Relationships

The most common reason for seeking the help of a medium is love. When we lose a loved one through death, we want to know if they continue to survive, if they are all right, if they are still in contact with us, and if the bond of love endures.

One of the most commonly communicated messages of the afterlife is that love is eternal. We congregate in the afterlife with a group of similarly minded souls at the same level of development. We remain closest with those with whom we have the strongest bond of love and the greatest affinity. My grandmother had an old colloquial saying that I have always liked, "Each to his own, said the old lady who kissed the cow."

My guide says,

> "Our common affinity and harmony, our deep bond of love and affection, holds us together. We don't maintain false relationships or facades based on deceit or false presumptions. A common bond holds us together. We stay with those with whom we had the greatest affinity and love. Those who have true,

deep, mutual love and affection and common goals stay together. People who didn't get along on earth or have a close relationship or love for one another don't spend much time together in the afterlife. They do not see much of one another or stay around each other. Their lack of affinity causes them to go separate ways.

We all have some people that we still see from earth, but it depends on how close we were to them. We see some people with more frequency than others. We are able to choose who we wish to be with. Some we are very close to. We form companionships, partnerships and friendships based on the degree of affinity and love. We think of ourselves as associates, friends, loved ones, and partners, some closer and some not close. As on earth, there are choices. We can be alone, stay with one, or stay with many. We can stay with one soul as a partner if we wish. We can separate and join another. We can even promise to be united forever. This is the closest thing we have to marriage on the other side. It is a serious spiritual commitment that two souls make to remain together and not be separated. We see it as a partnership or pairing."

The medium, Laurie, channeled her guides, "There definitely are pairings of spirits on the other side. They do refer to themselves as pairs, mates, couples, and unions. This is true on the third and fourth levels. "

There are no set roles in the afterlife. There is no set gender in the afterlife. We have all had multiple life times, been multiple genders, and played multiple roles in our various lifetimes. As there are no marriages or children born in the afterlife, there are no husbands, wives, parents, children, brothers or sisters. There is no need for the typical roles of husband and wife as there is no need for childrearing, housekeeping, or earning a living. No legal agreement is needed to bind people together for the sake of support or childrearing when they do not want to stay together. We are all just souls relating to one another with various degrees of closeness. We can assume the appearance of a specific gender if we like or relate to someone as a parent, child, husband, wife, brother, or sister and maintain that type of relationship if we like. We have our own choices of how we prefer to appear and how we wish to interact. The outside superficialities of our earth lives are no longer important. The deep bond of true love and commitment is. Those who have a true bond of love remain together. That bond is never broken.

A channeled message I have received from my guide is,

"There are no marriages on the other side. Marriage is an institution not only devised to allow two people to make a public commitment to being viewed as a family unit, but more so to insure that two people who do not love each other stay together. Two people who do love each other do not need a legal bond to force them to stay together or to fulfill responsibilities to wife, husband, or children.

As souls do not have a gender, no one has to fulfill a specific role. Souls do not bear children and there is no need to raise children. No one has to work for a living or to clean a house. Therefore, there is no need for the artificial roles of husband, provider, and wife, childrearer. There is therefore no need to force two people who don't love each other to stay together to fulfill responsibilities.

But for those souls who deeply love one another, a spiritual commitment can be made. It is referred to as union. Two souls can express a vow or commitment to remain united, in other words, to remain together throughout eternity. This is not a temporary or lifetime commitment like a marriage, but a deeper soul commitment, one that is intended to be permanent. Although souls have free will and always are free to separate, it is a way of making a solemn promise to one another."

Those who have had a very happy marriage on earth may choose to stay together. The medium, Robert Brown, channeled, "If that small spark of true love was there, they may choose to remain together and that love continues to grow on the other side. Otherwise they separate. "

My guide channels,

"We don't have to be with souls we do not want to be with. People who don't get along won't stay together. People are not forced to be together. We choose who we want to be with. We stay with those we love. If we had an unhappy marriage on earth, we are not required to stay with that soul. Most marriage unions on earth do not stay together. Few earthly marriages persist on the other side as companions. Most separate and follow their own paths, realizing why they were together on earth, what lessons they were supposed to learn from one another. We learn to forgive one another, some more quickly and others with time. We let go of our past mistakes, learn from them, and move on. We realize why we were with someone, assess what we have learned from the relationship, appreciate the wisdom we have gained, and move forward."

As the medium, Laurie, channeled, "If we were unhappy or incompatible with someone in our lifetime, we separate and see very little of each other in the afterlife ".
We appreciate the lessons we learned from that bad marriage. If we see that soul in the afterlife, we treat them with civility, cordiality, kindness, and consideration, and wish them well. We honor and respect one another, and treat each other with congeniality.
In one of her books, Toni Winninger channels a spirit, "Marriages, former wives and husbands from one lifetime are a very insignificant thing in the scheme of eternity."

My guide channels,

> "Although love involves concern or caring for another individual or individuals, there are different kinds of love or expressions of love. We have an agapeic, altruistic, or godly love, a concern, consideration, compassion, respect, and kindness toward all souls, wishing them growth, progress, and happiness. This is a godly, altruistic love, one that we have for all spirits, a desire for their welfare and growth, a respect and compassion or empathy. This is an all-embracing, cordial, well-wishing love, a kind and helpful concern for the well-being of others.
> We also have an individual love for particular souls with whom we have especially close bonds. These

are souls we are closer to with deeper love and affinity. This is a more personal love, a bond of affinity and deep personal love that holds people or spirits together through compatibility, deep love, and devotion. These are souls who wish to be together, whose mutual love, commitment, and deep intimacy, bond them together.

The concept of romantic love is a human one. Even though souls do not have a physical body, they can entertain or retain romantic feelings for another soul if they wish, if it is important to them. Although the biological drives are no longer present, souls can experience deep psychological needs or desires. If we had romantic feelings for someone on the earth, we can retain them on the other side if we wish. Our feelings of affection are more love-based and develop from love of the individual or character, rather than a temporary physical attraction. True unions are based on deep love for the essence or character of the person. Souls can experience passionate or sexual love together if they want. They can create the illusion of such a relationship and experience it in a way that feels real to them. If we have the desire or need for a physical type of relationship, for hugs and kisses, that wish can be fulfilled."

In her book, "*Karma I and II*", Shanna Spalding St. Clair channels this message, "Is there the physical or emotional sensation of love when one is in spirit? Whatever awareness is necessary for the progression of a soul in spirit will be made available to that soul (35)."

Raymond, Sir Oliver Lodge's son, channels, "Men and women can have the same feelings for each other on the other side but expressed in a different manner and stand in a slightly different relationship. You gravitate to ones you have affinity for-like attracts like. Spirits can also come over with earthly desires and can have what they want for a while (198). "

Gretchen Vogel channels, "Love is the key. People may have plenty of pre-deceased relatives, but if there was no love between them in life, there may be no abiding attachment in the afterlife either. Couples and pets often do stay together. I see many couples in the afterlife who are together and many who are not. We can stay together with those we love on earth, but it must be mutual (52). We can also stay near a loved one to serve as a guide or guardian (53, 83). ""Unconditional love comes from the mind (25)."

My guide states,

> "We have strong feelings of affection and love with some souls. We have companionships. We can see one another as pairs or couples."

Charlotte Dresser, in her book, channels, "Companionships on the other side are higher and finer and more enduring than worldly ties. Companionship is dependent on congeniality. Families do not often stay together. Each goes the way he prefers. There is not much importance to family ties. We are united more by congeniality. We are related by the thoughts we think, the ideas we cherish. The loves you develop are dearer and nearer then the ties of blood (Loc 2285, Kindle edition)." "We know our soul companions. Spirit meets its own. Your electromagnetic or vibrational signature calls persons of a similar attraction. We are attracted by the same thoughts, plans, desires, and tastes. We can come together with a soulmate and at last form a perfect union of wisdom and love (Loc 2295, Kindle edition)." "On this side not many are married in spirit and it is only in spirit that the tie continues (Loc 2295, Kindle edition)."

Jasper Swain, in "*The Death of my Son*", reports his son as saying, "Two souls merge in true spiritual union."

I discussed with my guide the attributes of a good relationship. These are the conclusions.

>A relationship should be a collaboration, not a contest. Both individuals need to be loving and caring. As we become accustomed to each other and integrate the responsibilities of our lives, we may lose some of the initial excitement of the relationship and develop a deeper union, coalescence, and compatibility , with peace, harmony, and contentment. Both parties need to work at developing that unity and harmony . Communication, compromise, and forgiveness are all important. Without the willingness to communicate, problems cannot be addressed, discussed, or solved and lack of communication builds a wall of separation which cannot be bridged. Both parties must be willing to talk things over. As no two individuals are identical, both need to compromise. Important decisions should be made jointly. In a good relationship, each has concern for the other's feelings and welfare. Both will be willing to share and compromise. The two parties should lift each other up. In a good union, both people help one another, sharing the responsibilities, and caring for one another, both physically and financially. They work together for the common benefit. Both also need to work at maintaining the passion, excitement, and joy of the relationship. If all the effort is one sided, the partner doing all of the giving will

tire of the relationship, and may seek satisfaction elsewhere. The more alike two people are physically and spiritually, the more compatible they are, the closer their relationship will be. They both need to agree on what they expect of a relationship and what their idea of love is. If they agree on what their idea of love is and are both willing to give and receive love, they can have a good relationship. Truthfulness, trust, and sincerity are important. If there is deceit or false pretense there is a bad relationship. If we love someone who is lying or deceitful, we love the person we imagine them to be in our mind, not the real person, because we don't know the real person. We may never have loved the real person, only the person we thought they were. Verbal abuse, disparaging or insulting comments, or physical abuse, indicate a bad relationship. Don't be concerned with petty things. Emotional expressiveness is important. Each should let the other know how much they care for and appreciate them demonstrating love and affection, being thankful for the love they have. Common interests and pursuits are important, cooperating and sharing common work, endeavors, interests and pleasures . Always work on unity, with a strong partnership of love, emotion, work, cooperation, affection, intellectual pursuits, recreation, and endeavor. Be one and think as one, not as two. Forgive, love, trust, and give. Make a happy relationship your top priority.

Twenty One

# Spirit Occupations and Recreation

We do have work of our own choosing based upon what we need to learn or what we desire to learn. We have occupations that are similar to those on the earth. We have people who build, design, and create. We have people who are dedicated to artistic endeavors. We have teachers and healers. We have those who are involved in the development of technology and a furthering of science. We have those who are involved in the well-being of the soul. We have those who assist, inspire, and influence workers on the earth. We have those who help other souls' progress. We continue to grow and advance, but not as dramatically or quickly as when we are in the negative and chaotic atmosphere of earth.

As Charlotte Dresser's book, "*Life Here and Hereafter*", states, "We have no need for food or money, buying or selling, no need of things money buys. There are no nuisances, robbers, thieves, no need for care of house or clothing. They who serve most are the greatest here (Loc 1688, Kindle edition)."

My guide indicates,

"We have no need for many of the occupations that we had on earth. We don't need jailers, cooks, or maintenance workers. We don't need salesman and bankers. We don't need merchants or doctors. We do have healers, helpers, teachers, builders, artists, designers and governing leaders .

We don't have criminals or violence. We don't have altercations or hostility. There is no destruction or murder. Although we may disagree, we learn to live in harmony, and each follows his own path. We learn to act civilly and respectfully with others. We don't have the negative feelings of the earth and are not compelled to stay with those with whom we are not compatible. We are not permitted to harm others. Anything that involves the body or things that are negative we don't need. Anything that involves the mind or things that are positive we have.

We get together socially and discuss topics of interest. We can pursue intellectual learning or become involved in creations of artistry and beauty. We can assume a humanoid type of body and participate in a sport or dance. We can create a scenario with our mind/imagination and live that scenario and it will seem real to us. We can create music, art, literature. We can travel, learn, watch shows, or participate in games if we wish. We laugh, we have comedies, music, arts, travel, education, and social camaraderie."

A relative of mine who has passed communicated to me through a group of mediums that he is seeking knowledge and learning in the afterlife but that knowledge is directly infused into our minds and we do not read books in the traditional fashion.

A very fine medium, Dorie, stated that her son, on the other side, told her that we have an energetic body similar to our humanoid body but of a finer, more ethereal substance and we can do similar things to what we did on the earth in our ethereal bodies, such as play tennis or golf.

My guide states that,

" We can travel further and do more than we could when in the physical body. We have no limitations of the physical kind. We do have laws that we adhere to. There are certain limitations of a spiritual nature, as on the earth we have natural laws. We are not able to move beyond a certain limit of speed. We don't progress beyond our level until we have learned or accomplished certain things. We are able to travel to other dimensions but not beyond our own limitations. We are able to travel to others who are at our own developmental level but are different. We are able to visit some that are more evolved. We are able to apprehend more than we could in the physical. We are not able to see all or know all that exists.

Not only is existence infinite in distance or space, it is also infinite in dimension or vibrational layers. We are able to travel farther than human ability would permit. We are able to visit others in the universe who are beyond human capability to reach. We can travel to or experience other dimensional states but not as many as those who are more highly evolved or developed."

A group of spirits channeling through the medium Karuna answered a question of mine as to whether there is the possibility of experiencing houses or buildings in the Spirit world. They answered, "It's interesting that this question has been asked many times of spirit and it is a question that is related to many other questions regarding familiarity. It is natural for a human to be concerned with comparisons. Do not be concerned for those aspects of life that bring security, safety and familiarity, for those will always be available to you. The security of knowing where home is, the appreciation of the beauty of architecture, all these aspects of humanity are available to those who desire these things which have been vital to them during some progression of their development. What you manifest through your thoughts is always available to you. Do not your thoughts become more powerful and stronger as you develop? Is not the creative process expanding forever? It is unlimited in its power. We say, perhaps the question should be are there any limitations to the creative process? And if the answer is no, that "no" can easily answer many questions having to do with comparisons between physical form and Spirit form. "

Twenty Two
# Love

International medium, Robert Brown, gave this communication through spirit. Speaking of husbands and wives, he said, "If that small spark of true love is present, they can choose to stay together. That love will continue to grow in the afterlife. Otherwise they will separate."

Love and service are emphasized by the communications of Charlotte Dresser.

St. Clair refers to "loving kindness" in "*Karma I and II*" as being of paramount importance (102).

The Bible states," Love is strong as death." I used to carry that clipping in my wallet when I was young. Little did I know how much that would mean to me one day.

Love is the strongest force in the universe. It builds bridges and opens up communication with the spirit world. It is eternal.

"*Karma I and II*" states, "You are never separated from those you love. There is always connection from soul to soul whether in spirit or in body for those who care for one another. There is no separation in spirit (49)." "Love connects. Love is the most powerful energy that exists for it is capable of providing great change. Understand love and all its aspects to perfect knowledge of your purpose and accomplishment (59)."

Claude, communicating from the afterlife in "*Claude's Second Book*," states, "There is always a link between the spirits of people who truly love each other (65)."

Frederick Sculthorpe, in his book, "*Excursions to the Spirit World*," states, "There is no real separation in spirit (20)."

The spirits communicating through Charlotte Dresser say, "Those linked by the strong bond of love, affection, and sympathy have psychic connection in proportion to the strength of these ties."

Gretchen Vogel channels, "Unconditional love comes from the mind (25)."

The white light of God is said to embody love, truth, compassion, loyalty, humility, patience, peace and joy.

Many people have reported telepathic communication from those they love, particularly in times of emotional distress, disaster, or death.

My guide states,

> "No one will lose someone they truly love. Love lasts forever. For those who truly love there will be no loss or heartache. We will be reunited with those we truly love. All the joy and happiness of eternal life and eternal love will be ours and the momentary pain and transient grief of our earthly lives will vanish and dissolve in tears of joy. No one can express the ineffable joy and peace of the everlasting love and happiness of two souls united in contentment and love."

The channeling of "*Karma I and II*" states, "Love has many forms (49)."

My guide channels,

"There is a godly or humanitarian love which is the love, kindness, and compassion we have for all souls on their individual paths. It is consideration and well wishes for their progression, growth, and happiness. All are to be treated with respect and consideration. There is a shared love between friends and siblings and the protective love of parents. There is the love of a child for a caregiving parent and the love of souls for their Creator. There is also a more personal love, the bond of affinity that souls who have a very deep personal love for one another and a desire to be together experience. This is the desire for a mate or companion."

Those who have visited the afterlife and returned in near death experiences state that it is a place of ineffable peace and love.

I dedicate this poem to my loved one, who is also now my guide, in the afterlife:

## LOVE

> It cannot be counted in watts or degrees,
> In centimeters or grams,
> It cannot be measured in mass or in force,
> Its amount no scale commands;
> It has no height, no depth, no size,
> No substance of its own,
> And only within its effect
> Is it's nature known;
> It has no life, it has no form,

PRUDENCE ANN SMITH M.D.

And yet is life's essence,
And, though unperceived, worlds
Are changed by its presence;
It has no bounds, it can't be seen,
Yet may be without end,
Freely given or received,
No man can buy or spend;
Not tasted, touched in any way
Known unto the sense,
It seems like nothing, yet no thing
Was ever so immense.

Twenty Three
# Soulmates and Twin Flames

Soulmates are souls that are part of a soul group or soul family. These are a group of souls who reincarnate together in various relationships on the earth plane to teach each other lessons. We have usually had many prior lifetimes together. As in an earth family, where we have both immediate and extended family members, some members of our soul group are closer than others and some are more distant.

In *"Karma I and II"*, St. Clair describes this type of soulmates as karmic task mates. We are each teaching and learning from one another.

Because we are part of a soul group does not mean we all have harmonious relationships. We may be more or less compatible, and have negative relationships with some and positive relationships with others. We interact with one another to mutually promote advancement and progression. Some may be our closest companions, who are like-minded and supportive. We may have an antagonistic or tumultuous relationship with others. In either case, we collaborate to mutually aid one another in our growth.

We have a small circle of close associates, and larger groups of interacting souls. Our contacts branch out like the limbs on a family tree. We are also able to have relationships with and convene with souls on our level outside of our immediate soul group in the afterlife. Not everyone we encounter in our lifetime on earth is a part of our soul group. However, most of the major interactions we have in our lifetime, partnerships, family, and significant relationships, are with those from our soul group. Oftentimes, someone who precipitates a major change in your life or seems familiar is a part of your soul family.

Souls on the other side are able to dwell together, maintain houses together, work together, and take care of one another at their own discretion.

Not all soulmates have to incarnate in each incarnation simultaneously. Some may remain behind in the afterlife for a given incarnation. When a soul group plans to incarnate, the members mutually make agreements and contracts with one another to provide certain situations that will allow the members to learn the lessons they need to learn. Soul groups vary in size, and although numbers are not hard and fast, typically range from 25 through 150 souls. They usually incarnate in a group and incarnation can occur at any interval, but frequently occurs at a span between 80 and 120 earth years.

Alternatively, there is the option of remaining in the afterlife and not incarnating on the earth. Souls may elect this option, but they can progress and learn more quickly in the dense and negative environment of the earth.

Kindred souls include the many souls that we have known in one or multiple past lifetimes. These are souls of a similar nature that we have interacted with.

There is a special soulmate relationship known as twin flames. These are two souls created or broken off from Source at the same time, who are very similar in identity, essence, character, disposition, and nature. They are a pair of souls that are like twins in an emotional, intellectual, and spiritual sense. They are souls who are so close they do not often wish to be separated. They are almost like two halves of a whole and share such a close affinity that they are happiest when they are together and often share the closest of bonds. They feel incomplete or unfulfilled without one another. They are exceptionally close, in fact, the closest of soulmates. Having the closest of bonds, they may become united, proclaiming a spiritual commitment of union with one another.

We are more closely connected to a twin flame than to any other soul. They are the male and female aspects of one another. They frequently serve as guardians to one another, one remaining in the afterlife and guiding the other through their earthly incarnation to assist each other in maintaining an equal level of development. "*Karma I and II*" describes these soulmates and states that at the end of their incarnations they reunite with one another as one soul. Reportedly, they usually incarnate separately since they spend an eternity together on the other side.

My personal experience is that once you have felt that kind of love for someone, you will always be searching for it, never fully content without it.

Twenty Four
# Union

Spiritual commitment is also possible in the afterlife, although marriage is not practiced as upon earth. The earthly marriage bond can be a spiritual bond, but often is just a legal bond that holds people who do not love one another together for the sake of raising children or for reasons of financial security and obligation. Since children are not born in the afterlife, souls do not have a gender, and the traditional roles of husband as breadwinner and wife as homemaker are not applicable, a legal marriage is not needed.

One communicator from the other side regarded marriage on earth more as a procedure for organized living than as a sacred ceremony. He stated that oftentimes the young bind themselves irrevocably to a condition beyond their experience. He described some unions as failures, as two people who made an initial error, now forcibly maintained in the closest of contacts, and disagreeing, no longer loving one another, injuring one another and possibly others.

Regarding life on the other side, Walter Scott, in his book, "*As One Ghost to Another* ", states, "Unions can approach the ideal and justify monogamy. These unions are probably eternal, better than the best moments on earth. You will not lack for perfect companionship or search without rest for completion. Unions made in the afterlife ultimately prove as happy as the best on earth. They grow together. They help each other in spiritual advancement, each raising the other to further heights. "

However, souls who wish to establish or celebrate a bond between each other can proclaim a spiritual union, a commitment to remain together throughout eternity, if they wish. Such loving bonds are performed by stating or proclaiming such a bond to one another in the Akashic records.

My guide states,

> "Most unions on earth are the result of physical attraction and are ephemeral. Souls in the afterlife unite due to true inner compatibility. This is a compatibility of the inner personality or soulprint, which is spiritual. Beautiful unions are eternal. The souls in such a union grow together and help each other in perfect companionship and completion of one another. We are able to be together with those we love deeply and we are able to become united with those we wish to remain with. As such, we have unions, alliances, partnerships, pairings of like-minded, loving souls who wish not to be separated throughout eternity."

A channeled message through the medium, Karuna, states, "Some souls have been together for eons and eons ".

Charlotte Dresser, channeling a soul communicating from the afterlife, describes a soul arriving in the afterlife who discovers that a married couple she had known on earth were no longer together. "Each goes to his own place where his congeniality is expressed. Not many keep together here. Not many are married in spirit and it is only in spirit that the tie continues on this side. Comparatively few keep that tie here. Most are happier to go their own way. They find their mates at last and come into perfect happiness. "

Twenty Five
# Source

Souls on the other side acknowledge that there is a higher power that is the source of all that is, from which everything originates. Those souls on the lower levels of the afterlife say that they have never seen or met God. Some children, returning from near death experiences, claim to have met Jesus or angels. One thing is certain. We did not create ourselves.

It seems apparent that souls on the lower planes of the afterlife agree, or are more sure that there is a God. Some regard God as an impersonal force, and others regard God as a more personalized or individualized creator of the kind referred to in the Bible. Other mediums also speak of having contacted Ascended Masters, or Angels and Archangels.

I believe that there is a scale of development and multiple varying manifestations of spirit, as there are many varying types of men on the earth, from those who are martyrs or saints, those who are devoted to a humanitarian life, and those who are devoted to criminal activity and harming others.

I had a unique opportunity to ask several spirits I knew well in life about religion and God since they have passed. One is a minister and his wife, whom I knew for many years. He spoke through several mediums I know. I asked him whether religion and things on the other side are like he believed when he was on earth. He replied, "That is a loaded question. Some things are the same as I believed, but I was surprised by others. The religious beliefs we had on earth were a comfort and a help to us, and helped to guide our lives in a good and positive direction." He was a Christian in a very devoted fundamentalist group. Although he didn't specify what surprised him and what was as he believed, I suspect that he probably found truth in his moral beliefs and kind and devoted works, but perhaps had a broader and less sectarian view of religion when he transitioned to the other side.

I had the opportunity to speak to a relative of mine who had passed. We used to read the Bible together and used to discuss and conjecture about what we thought the afterlife might be like. I had the opportunity to ask him through several mediums. He said' "It is even better than we imagined." He imparted a feeling to one of the mediums he came through who is very clairsentient, and she remarked, "If that's how he feels, I want to be where he is."

My guide also overlaid his feelings on me one day. I barely have words for what I felt. The feeling was of extreme exhilaration and joy, indescribable happiness, almost rapture, well-being, love, and lack of fear.

My guide channels,

> "People all have their own beliefs about God. We don't know God like we would know another person. We do not have an idea of what God looks like. We all believe that God or a creator, or creative force exists. We know that God exists from the continuation of life.

God is the ultimate source of all that is. God is the divine origin of life.

God has attributes as those of other spirits, the ability to love, to help, to create.

I do believe that God has a set of principles or morals, a right and wrong governing of behavior. We do not have the permission or ability to hurt, harm, or injure other souls. We do have certain levels of development that apply to our understanding and behavior. We do have advanced souls who advise us on spiritual growth.

We don't have separate denominations if we are advanced. We just have an understanding of moral principles. We don't have need for sects and divisions. Our principles are ones that are universal. We look toward God with gratitude and joy. We better understand the love of God. We don't have hatred, harm, prejudice, or lies. We realize that there is a code of behavior embodied in helping others, unselfish service, kindness, forgiveness, and a desire not to willfully harm others. There are advanced souls who visit us, and they do seem to understand more deeply the attributes of God.

I think of God as a wonderful, loving creator, the origin of all spirit. I feel God is a spirit, an intelligent, loving creator. I feel that the creative force has identity and consciousness, intelligence and emotion, and loves us. God is the spirit that is in us, only perfected."

If we as spirits in a human form broke off from God as some books say, then we must be a spirit, like God. From this we could draw the conclusion that a part of the spirit of God is within each of us. That is what we call the life force, the part of us that survives death.

I reason, does it make sense to regard God or Source as a blind force? Does it make sense that a blind force can give rise to souls who have identity, consciousness, intelligence, and personality? Does it make sense that something without identity can create something with identity? That something without consciousness would create something with consciousness? That something without the capacity to love could create something that loves? Is the creation greater than the creator? That doesn't make sense. If God is a spirit as we are spirits, then God must also have the attributes of spirits.

The Bible states that God is a spirit and seeks those to worship Him in truth and in spirit. If God is the source of unconditional love, if there is progression of souls and a spiritual hierarchy with evolution, masters, angels, etc., then there must be a purpose in our lives, a goal and an objective to grow toward. If we learn lessons and have a life review, there must be a right and a wrong way of behavior, or way of thinking that we aspire to. If God teaches and practices unconditional love, God must be an intelligent spirit with identity, feelings, and personality, not a blind force.

I feel that God is a very powerful source of creation, God is not just a blind force. God is an intelligent, loving creator. God is more than just a power. God is like us, a consciousness, a strong, loving intelligent spirit, the creator, the source of all that is.

Shanna Spalding St. Clair, in her book, "*Karma I and II*", channels the attributes of God. She states, "The white light of God embodies loyalty, honesty, unity, compassion, and truth, the highest qualities attainable in human form."

Twenty Six
# Negative Spirits

There is no doubt that on earth many people demonstrate negative behavior. Look at the serial killers and the many criminal acts that are perpetrated against others. I asked my guide about negative souls or spirits.

He answered,

"A soul who is negative is not created negative. Spirits are not inherently negative. Spirits who are negative choose to be. They can take on negative thoughts and actions on the earth. They have entered into a negative state because of their earth lives. They have adopted a negative persona. They are not permanently negative by definition. No soul has to be negative. We all have free will of choices. We can be negative because we were in a negative situation or made negative choices. We can choose reactions that are negative, harmful, or detrimental to ourselves and other souls. That is part of the earth lesson-learning to make positive choices.

We can be negative in our thoughts or actions, or both. We can choose to change if we desire to change. No one is negative permanently unless they want to be. The opportunity to change is always there for us. They need to learn to take off or pull off negativity. But if less developed, they may choose negativity when in situations or conditions where negativity can be expressed. They have the propensity to be negative and the lack of development, causing them to stay negative. Therefore, that spirit is at a lower vibrational level or developmental stage and needs to progress and learn.

We don't have a negative environment on the other side, so there is no need for negativity. Souls may stay negative for a while, but will not remain negative if they step into the light. After they cross over, they may retain negative thoughts and feelings for a while. They have the ability to act negative again if they return to earth. A soul will reverse as much negativity as possible the more it attempts to choose the positive over the negative in subsequent incarnations as opportunities arise. It depends on whether they have learned their lessons.

Souls gravitate to different levels of development, different vibrational levels, based upon their vibration or level of development. In this manner we select our own place in the afterlife by the life we live on earth and the choices we make. These reflect our character and determine our placement on graduation day. Through development and subsequent positive choices throughout many incarnations we can overcome negativity.

Souls can have inherent weaknesses that they discover when they come to earth and have the opportunity to act in bad or negative ways. They do not have the ability or opportunity to act in those same negative ways on the other side. When we experience what our weaknesses cause both in harm to ourselves and others, we are guided to overcome them and make better choices.

Those who have passed can feel all of the emotions we as humans feel, including the negative ones such as anger, sadness, or violence. We can still relive the negative emotions if we bring back memories of the unhappy parts of our prior earth lives. But when we cross over and no longer have to be in a bad marriage, work at a job we dislike, or have to suffer ill health and physical pain, aren't the victims of injustice, theft, or physical harm, don't have to suffer lies, abuse, or mistreatment, don't have to live in poverty or struggle to live, the negatives are no longer relevant, important, or needed. When we don't live under bad circumstances, depression, anger, frustration, and unhappiness are no longer pertinent."

A message channelled by the soul group Abraham through the physical and mental medium, Karuna, states, "We do not always become instantly positive in the afterlife if we have had a very negative mind set in our incarnation. It can take some time to release negativity and become positive. It is easier to be positive in the afterlife environment surrounded by love and helpfulness and without the negative things happening to us that happened on earth. "

My cousin, Barbie Mines, who lost her life at a young age in a tragic accident, speaking through a medium, states, "We do not instantly become perfect when we die. The negative emotions from our earth lives can bleed through to the other side. There is still some drama on the other side. "

When my mother was communicating with me through a medium, I asked how we get along with those in the afterlife with whom we had hurtful or difficult relationships on earth. She said, "The mountains become evened out and become little hills. We make peace. We understand why we had an earth life together and what we were supposed to learn from each other."

Gretchen Vogel, in her book, "*Choices in the Afterlife,* "states, "Spirits work to rid themselves of all emotions that are not helpful or productive. They choose to cultivate, practice, and sustain positive emotions (69, 107). "

My guide states that spirits can have unresolved issues or unfinished business, so things aren't always resolved instantaneously on the other side. Medium Kim Russo says, "If business isn't resolved and worked through on this side, and let go of, spirits can carry it into the next life. "

I have often wondered when people commit negative acts in this life whether they were planned by contract in the afterlife before they came to earth for us to learn from or the result of free will when we get to the earth. In Toni Wininger's books, spirits have come through stating that they made contracts with other spirits when planning a life on earth to commit negative acts that all would learn from. A spirit stating that he was Hitler in his lifetime on earth claimed that he had deliberately chosen to act maliciously so that people on earth could learn of and see the horrors of evil. I wondered about this.

I have been told that some acts are planned for us to learn from and grow. We learn even from painful experiences. Perhaps we learn the most from difficult and unpleasant experiences. Other acts I was told, are spontaneous, and a result of free will.

Charlotte Dresser, in her book, *"Life Here and Hereafter"*, states that, "Spirits can be malicious after they die (Loc 195, Kindle edition)."

Some of the popular ghost shows on television talk about demons. One medium I know of does not believe in the existence of demons. Others do.

My guide states,

> "There are demons. They are negative creative forces that inhabit the lower levels of existence, not the light. They are creatures who choose negativity, preferring darkness to light. They were not ever human. They dwell in the lower levels of the world of spirit. They were not created evil, but chose evil and inflict harm."

People have reported negative, harmful spirits or demons invoked through devil worship.

In one place in the Bible, it states that we wrestle not with flesh and blood, but against spiritual wickedness in high places. Whatever your belief may be, I believe there is a good and a bad, a positive and a negative, a beneficent and a malevolent. People demonstrate that with their actions. After all, we are spirits in a human body having a human experience. Whatever name you give to it, there are negative and positive spiritual attitudes, actions, and choices.

Advice I received from my guide on the other side regarding negativity is as follows.

> "We all have undergone negative situations. You have to look for the positive in the negative. What

did I learn from this situation that made me unhappy? How will I be able to handle it better the next time? Am I trying to live right despite the wrongs visited upon me? What can I do to help others and help myself? Am I being true to what my heart tells me? Can I live and be able to say I did something worthy with my life? Did I help others to move forward and move myself forward? Did I act in a way that was in accordance with the best interests of others and my own best interest?

If a situation is negative, you should try to reach a compromise that is in the best interest of all concerned. Attempt to fulfill obligations and responsibilities while preserving some happiness for yourself. Try to find the best compromise possible to meet the needs of yourself and others.

Be as kind as you can under the circumstances. Don't compromise you're integrity. Love with a true heart. Don't believe in all limits. Believe that you are able to surmount some. Try to lift others and yourself. Be as strong and positive as you can. Take the next step. Don't rest on your laurels or become complacent. Be as truthful as you can with this in mind, that you want others to be truthful with you."

Twenty Seven

# Akashic Records

The Akashic Records are like a spiritual database, the eternal record of each soul's existence and prior lives. The records are kept in a spiritual or an ethereal medium and can be accessed by guides, teachers, and advanced souls participating in our development. Even we can access the portion of our own Akashic Record that will aid us in our current incarnation.

The records are an eternal preservation of every soul's progress and contain every thought, feeling, statement, or deed that soul has done. When we cross over at the transition called death we undergo a life review. This is a critique of our most recent life. In it we see major interactions we have had with other souls, acts we have committed, things we have said, and the reactions other people had to what we did and said. We see the reactions of others and feel the pain we caused others. It is a self assessment that can be quite painful. As the Bible said, "What is done in the dark will come to the light". All of us will go through this process.

We will also review what we had planned to learn before we came to earth and assess what we learned and didn't learn. We also have the opportunity to discuss our past life with other souls we interacted with, discussing what we might or should have done and why we did what we did. We are able to extrapolate the " what if's" and decide how we might better have approached some of the problems we encountered. We can also decide what we should have done or what we would do if we were placed in that situation again.

A book entitled, *"What Tom Sawyer Learned from Dying"* explains that a man named Tom Sawyer, in going through the life review after he died, relived an incident he had in his lifetime where he punched a drunk man who got in his way and was acting surly. This time he relived the incident from the drunk man's point of view. The man had just lost his wife and was emotionally distressed and inebriated. Tom Sawyer felt the blows he had inflicted on the man, the man's shame, anger, and pain, and saw the same incident from that man's point of view.

Frederick WH Myers, communicating from the afterlife, says, "We become aware of all the emotions of those we have hurt, the victims."

I know that the Akashic Records are real and that the life review is real. As I said earlier, I had suffered a very painful loss of a loved one and was devastated. Because of that loss I decided to change my life. I wanted to correct the things I had done wrong and become a better person. I had already been communicating with my loved one in spirit, but what came next was quite a surprise. When I realized that we had scripted our lives before we came to earth to learn lessons, I heard the words in my mind, "Now we can tell you." I received a life review that went on for nearly 24 hours. Luckily I didn't have to go to work the next day. My spirit guides spoke to me almost non-stop. This was a verbal recitation of many personal details of my life that I could not stop. They presented to me every wrong thing I had done, said, or thought in my lifetime. Many of the things brought to my attention I hadn't even remembered. Some I didn't think were wrong when I did them, but I was informed of why they were. It was shocking to say the least.

This was an extremely humbling experience. I could not turn the voices off. I tried. So I knew this wasn't coming from my own thoughts. It felt almost like a police inquisition. I was exhausted when it was over. I never felt so bad in my life. I felt shame and regret. For weeks I was so humiliated I was barely able to speak with my guides. As painful as it was, it was a blessing, allowing me to recognize my misdeeds and thoughts, to correct some of my actions before I cross over. Before this occurred, I had expressed a desire to change my entire life to do things better, to not repeat the mistakes I had made. This experience was given to me as a blessing and kindness, allowing me to change my life for the better.

Twenty Eight

# Forgiveness

My guide comments,

"We learn to forgive. We don't remain angry. We realize that we came to earth and experienced certain situations to learn from them. We respect and appreciate those who contributed to our development. Some can forgive the insults of their physical lives instantaneously and others require more time.

Even those who played negative roles in our lives we come to respect and thank for the difficult lessons we learned from them and the part they played in our progression. After all, we chose this life and these lessons for ourselves, even the difficult ones, to learn from. How could I be angry at something I, myself, planned?"

In Shanna Spalding St. Clair's book, " *Karma I and II*", the comment is made, some things we cannot learn except through tragedy. We must learn to be grateful for all of our lessons no matter how painful they may be. All of them provide us an opportunity to learn and grow which we would not have otherwise had.

We learn more from difficult situations than happy ones. This does not mean we stay together in the afterlife with those with whom we were at odds or were incompatible. We appreciate the lessons that we learned from them and go our separate ways.

As one medium put it, if that small spark of true love is there, we can choose to stay together. Otherwise we separate.

Another medium, Laurie, said that those we didn't like or get along with in our earth lives, those we were incompatible with, we don't see much of in the afterlife.

We obviously can't spend an equal amount of time with all souls. We remain with those with whom we have a deep mutual love and compatibility.

My mother came through a medium and answered a question for me at a circle. I had wondered how we feel towards those we had difficulties with in life when we get to the other side. She said the mountains become leveled off and are small hills.

My cousin, Barbie Mines, who passed tragically at an early age, channeled to me through a medium in the Bahamas. She answered a question I had in my mind which the medium didn't even know I was asking. She said, "Some of the feelings and conflicts we have with others can bleed through into the afterlife. We don't always agree just because we are in the afterlife. There is still some drama here."

She also recently showed me the other side of the coin-forgiveness. She recently came through in a development circle and brought through her father. I don't think either one of them would mind my including this in the book. She had had a difficult relationship with her father on the earth plane, but has since made peace with him in the afterlife, and over time, has repaired the relationship. He came through to state his regret for some of his actions while he was alive on earth and indicates that he has changed on the other side, becoming a better person, as we all hope to do. That is the reason for our earth lives-to become better people ourselves and encourage others to become better people.

In other words, we forgive, make peace, and have a better understanding of the differences. Small hills may remain, that is, we may agree to disagree in our ideas. However, we harbor no bitterness or resentment. We don't necessarily choose to stay together or spend time together with those not in harmony with us, but we don't retain grudges. We get over it, make peace, and go our own ways.

Through the loss of my loved one, one of the things I have done is to forgive anyone who has done me wrong in my lifetime. After I realized how wrong I have been, I realized that I have caused myself more pain than anyone else has. If I ask and hope to be forgiven for what I have done, certainly I can forgive others the wrong they have done me.

Twenty Nine

# Heaven

None of the souls who have communicated to me have told me that they have met or seen God or Source. They have told me that they exist in a beautiful idyllic environment of love, and are much happier than they were on the earth. When I asked him what it was like, one deceased relative told me it is even more beautiful than we thought.

A deceased friend and former minister and his wife, said that some things were as they expected and some were a surprise.

None of us on the earth plane, except, perhaps, for those who have had near death experiences of a beautiful place with deceased loved ones, has any proof of what the next world is like.

From what I have been told and experienced myself I can infer the existence of a loving Creator.

Everything I have read or been told points to the fact that we have choices. Charlotte Dresser indicates that we look solid to each other. *"Karma I and II"* says that our form is transmutable, the environment more plastic, and we can change our form at will. Laurie's guides indicate that we inhabit a humanoid form, but without the internal organs, which are not needed. Charlotte Dresser indicates that we can create touch and feeling so we can hug and kiss if we want. Laurie's guides say that we transfer thought but we can have words if we want them. They also state that it is easier to recreate the sense of touch and sexual passion at some levels in the afterlife than it is at others. We can have a passionate, sexual relationship because we create an illusion, and while we are experiencing it, it is real to us. It is not just a memory. In the spirit or energetic form touch is not like touching skin. It is sensing vibrations.

My guide told me when I asked him if he was happier in the afterlife than on earth and if he missed anything on earth,

> "We have greater happiness here than we had on earth. The negatives of our earth lives are gone. There is no struggling to earn a living or doing an unpleasant job. There is no necessity to stay in an unhappy marriage. Others cannot harm us, lie to us, or steal from us. We have no sicknesses or pain of aging. I am much happier than I was on earth. In addition to this, all of the things we didn't complete on earth we can complete on the other side. Everything you wanted you will have."

My guide and loved one communicated these statements not only to me, but to two other mediums in different states who didn't know each other. The statements were identical. I did not provide leading questions. They were spontaneously given.

Charlotte Dresser, in *"Life Here and Hereafter"*, channels, "If we want something we loved or didn't have in life, as long as we didn't wish to harm others, we will not be denied that experience."

Gretchen Vogel, in her book, *"Choices in the Afterlife"*, states, "Everything we can imagine after death is possible to experience to some extent, if only within our mental reality (73, 145)."

Shanna Spalding St. Clair channels in her book, "*Karma I and II*", "You ask if there is the physical or emotional sensation of love when one is in spirit. Whatever awareness is necessary for the progression of a soul in spirit will be made available to that soul. In spirit, one creates one's own reality (35)." "There will be no separation in spirit for those who love, for those who care for one another (Sculthorpe, 25)."

The medium, Laurie's guides said "We serve a good Creator. If we need something it would be provided for us. It would be made possible. God can make anything happen."

Even though I don't know what occurs in the more advanced levels of the afterlife, that sounds like Heaven to me.

Thirty
# Paranormal Investigation

As there are many different opinions on mediumship and the reality of life after death, so there are many different opinions on paranormal investigation. Recent television shows have popularized paranormal investigation and the various devices used to attempt to document communication with spirits.

Although these investigations are commonly regarded as attempts to communicate with ghosts, communication is also possible with spirits who have crossed over into the light. Ghosts have been defined as earthbound spirits, but are not technically bound. They are spirits who have chosen for one reason or another to remain near the earth. Some have remained for unfinished business, for revenge, for love of a particular place such as a home or place of employment, because they are confused, or because they passed quickly or tragically and do not know how to cross over.

At times they can generate enough energy and learn how to make their presence known to the living. They can do this by manifesting visually as an apparition, by being heard or sensed, or by a moving or manipulating physical objects and electrical devices. People have even sometimes reported being touched or scratched. Familiar or unusual smells have been reported as well.

As in the physical world that we know, where people can be negative or positive, likewise spirits can be negative or positive. Some are protectors and others can be malicious with intent to harm.

I went on an investigation of the Queen Mary, a ship that is known to be haunted, now docked in the Los Angeles area, with a young, well known medium, A. J. Barrera. The group that I went with was comprised of all mediums, and we were allowed into areas that were off limits for the public tour.

We were admitted to the swimming pool area, the engine room, the area of the bow, the propeller room, several areas that contained memorabilia of the ship's past and those who had served on the ship, as well as a room that had been sealed shut after a man killed his entire family and then himself.

Some of us were able to communicate directly with several of the spirits. I was told by one that many of the spirits did not remain continuously in that location, but travelled back and forth to assist in communication with the living, to help promote awareness of life after death, and to commemorate those who had served or died on the ship.

A.J. brought along an array of paranormal investigation equipment. Phenomena were documented with full spectrum cameras, digital recorders, an SB 7 spirit box, which is a modified radio that allows you to program an AM or FM radio frequency sweep at various speeds in forward or reverse. Spirits can use these energies and frequencies and manipulate them to produce words that can be heard by the human ear. He also brought along an Ovilus, a device which uses different levels of energy and frequency, each paired to a word in an internal dictionary. Spirits can use their energy in a particular level or frequency to select a word from the dictionary, and an internal synthesizer will reproduce that word audibly.

Intelligent responses and activity were demonstrated through the Ovilus and SB 7 spirit box. This was especially true in the room that had been sealed since the prior, homicide/suicide. Quite a few responses were obtained and recorded.

In several rooms I captured photographs of many orbs. These were not particles of dust, and had a characteristic appearance of texture and defined inner detail. They were of different sizes and appeared throughout the rooms. I know personally that orbs exist and that they are not all faked or fabricated technologically because I obtained them with my own camera. I did not alter the digital images in any way. One appeared on my shoulder in one of the photographs, and I believe that was my guide, who was with me at the time. Seeing and experiencing for yourself is believing.

From going on several paranormal investigations, I gained a respect for spirits. After all, we are just spirits in a human body, and they, like us, are individuals and souls. We wouldn't like a group of people barging uninvited into our homes and asking us questions. In many instances, neither do they. Some dwell or reside in those locations and do not like to have their privacy violated. Others can be welcoming and social and enjoy the communication. Still others are teaching spirits, and look forward to the experience.

One pet peeve I have is that some people on television programs refer to a spirit as "it", or a "thing" rather than a spirit or soul. I have deceased loved ones, and I would never refer to them as "things" or "it", just because they have passed on.

I also personally do not like provocation. I understand that some investigators use it when they are not getting responses, to agitate the spirits so that they will respond. I wouldn't like it if someone were yelling at me or insulting me. As they are spirits as we are, only without the physical body, but otherwise the same, I can understand that they wouldn't like it either. I prefer to treat them with respect as I also would like to be treated with respect. My grandmother used to have a saying, "You catch more flies with honey than you do with vinegar."

I learned this when I was on an investigation of a historical church and museum in the Los Angeles area. I went into a room called the groom's room where grooms would prepare themselves before their wedding. Other investigators and visitors were known to become physically ill or nauseated when they sat in a particular chair in that room. As I went in, I began to talk with the spirit named George that supposedly resided there. I heard the answer that he liked his privacy and felt that all of the commotion was an intrusion. I respected his wishes and apologized for disturbing him, and I even got a visit from him the next morning as he said a few words to me, thanking me for my regard of his feelings and wishing me well. I learned a lesson that day and I have not been on an investigation for disturbances since that time. I am not condemning those who wish to investigate to obtain evidence of life after death, to help spirits move on and cross over into the light, or to help people who have mischievous or disturbing activity in their homes or workplaces. I merely feel that the investigative aspect of paranormal research in terms of ghost hunting, as it has been called, is not for me.

I am a gadget person. I enjoy experimenting with technology and equipment. I purchased some of the devices the paranormal teams use to document spirit activity. These include a SB 7 spirit box, an Ovilus, a REM pod /shadow detector, an RT EVP recorder, a full spectrum camera, a MEL meter with temperature alert, and a GEO phone vibration detector with LED light indicators. As I mentioned earlier, I saw some of these devices used by the psychic medium A.J. Barrera, who also lectured us in the Bahamas and demonstrated a variety of equipment. I planned to use them in a different manner, however.

I recently took my equipment to a weekend session at a friend's house. I reasoned that if spirits can communicate through these devices, perhaps in the presence of a physical medium, even greater activity could be documented. My friend, Karuna, as I indicated previously, is a talented physical and mental medium. In addition to channeling spirits and spirit groups from the other side, she has been able to produce phenomena in my presence, such as table tipping and movement, as well as the deflection of a compass needle in response to questions asked with yes and no answers. I have personally witnessed these phenomena and know they were genuine, not fabricated.

Various pieces of equipment that have been used in the past include the Ouija Board, a table which can move or tip, and a pendulum, which can be used to swing side to side or forward and backward, or to rotate clockwise or counterclockwise, to signify yes or no. Dowsing rods can also be used or manipulated by spirits to cross for yes or to open up wide for no. They can be made out of simple metal coat hangers. As with all communication devices, caution should be exercised. As you would not invite any stranger to come into your home, you should not invite just any spirit to communicate through these instruments. Your never know who may come to visit. You could be inviting a malicious entity in. It is important to ask your guides to remain close to you and to serve as a gatekeeper, allowing only those with the highest intention and messages of the greatest good for all concerned, through.

Our spirit circle also begins a session with an opening prayer and the request that we all are protected by the white light of God or Source. Whatever your preferred method, protection should be invoked.

For those who are skeptics, you must experience these phenomena and decide for yourself. Although there is more equipment than ever producing documented phenomena, the source of these phenomena must be determined by the person who experiences them. I know as surely as I know my own name that what I have experienced personally is true. I also firmly believe that the origin of these communications is in the spiritual world, and that I am truly speaking with those I love and with others who have passed on.

I brought along with me the equipment to see how useful it would be in the presence of a physical medium and see whether I could document any physical phenomena. The vibration detector, spirit box, and Ovilus III were active and produced results which I recorded with a digital recorder. My friend received answers through the Ovilus that were specific to and appropriate to the questions she asked. Several individuals she had known in her youth communicated. One was a scientist, whose name came through the box, with the word Pluto. This was an entirely appropriate response, as the individual had been an astrophysicist. The words that come through the Ovilus are individual words, and not complete sentences. Therefore, they are a kind of shorthand. Spirits must select them judiciously to establish a sparse, compact, intelligent response.

In a prior situation this same friend and myself had used the SB 7 spirit box. She was passing through town on her way home and I had just received the box. She wanted to see it, so I brought it along to a Chinese restaurant where we were having dinner. I turned the volume down so as not to disturb the other customers and we had a spirit box session right there in the restaurant. It was amazing. Neither of us had personally used the SB 7 spirit box before, but we got it working and, low and behold, intelligent responses started coming to the questions she asked.

One of these gave the name of her daughter and some personal information that let her know the communication was legitimate. Another question she asked was , "Do you know or see what we are doing?" The response immediately came back through the spirit box, "Soup." This was incredible as we had just been served a large family-style, bowl of soup. Our session in the restaurant was a great introduction.

While I was at my friend's home, I also videotaped a channeling session. We were attempting to document physical mediumship manifestations and to record channeled messages. I brought along a full spectrum camera which had been modified to record light waves in the infrared and ultraviolet wave length ranges, as well as visible spectrum light. We had infrared and ultraviolet flood lights.

Evidently I was not the first to think of this application for investigative equipment, as my friend, Karuna, had just returned from physical mediumship training at Arthur Findlay College in England. She described how they had set up an infrared camera as well as a K2 meter and other equipment to document any physical manifestations during the training session.

My friend had constructed a cabinet for physical mediumship in her den. I set up the camera, the K2 meter, and the geophone vibration detector in front of the cabinet. I didn't obtain any recordings of mists, orbs, or apparitions. I attribute this to the fact that my friend is in development in this area of ability. I understand that historically many mediums in Europe have to sit in circle with other individuals providing energy, sometimes for years, in order to develop this unique ability.

However, the recorded trance channeling sessions were remarkable, and provided interesting, intelligent, and sophisticated answers to questions that I asked.

With my participation and experimentation with equipment, I have come to the conclusion that spirits can communicate more detailed messages more efficiently through a human medium than they can through these devices. They expend more energy communicating through these devices, and are only able to communicate a few words at a time through the Ovilus, SB 7 spirit box, or EVP recorder. In other words, they must use more energy to get a shorter result. These devices and instruments are very good for providing hard and documentable evidence of spirit communication and they are also useful for those who have not developed mediumistic ability to communicate themselves.

Through other mediums and through myself I have received more complicated, lengthy, detailed, and personal messages and evidence of life after death and the survival of those I love. This has been the most efficient means of communication for me. In other words, each method has a particular use and value. The extra demonstrations provided by instruments and devices are valuable as well, and accepted with gratitude.

The first time I turned on my new Ovilus, I spoke with my guide and loved one in spirit and said, "I love you ". The first word I heard in response through the Ovilus was, "Hug." The next was, "Sent", followed by "Kiss" and Squeeze". Needless to say, I love my new Ovilus.

Thirty One

# Memorable Messages

I had one amazing reading from a group of mediums that meet with me on Sundays via Skype. We live in geographically different areas and can get together easily on the computer.

In some training classes, such as those of Lisa Williams, we are encouraged to bring through at least 3 specific evidential pieces of information or "direct hits "identifying a spirit.

In one Skype session, two of the mediums who did not know my former relative, as he was deceased before I met them, brought through an unbelievable number of direct hits. I had never discussed him with them, nor did they know any of my relatives, most of whom are also deceased. Here are some of the confirmations they gave me and the explanations I have added.

They said he was a musician, played in smoky bars and clubs, loved music, was seen tapping his foot as he played, was capable of playing more than one instrument, one of which he blew (a harmonica), there was a lot of applause for his music, he played jazzy music, also worked with his hands (in a machine shop). At times he could be focused and indifferent (practicing the guitar). They saw drums around him (I played the drums).He liked nature (He grew up in a rural setting and always liked getting out of the city and into the open fields). They described his physique, his paunchy stomach, his skin tone, his hair loss, his favorite hat, and the many baseball caps he wore. They said he smoked a pipe at one time. They said he was talkative, loved to communicate, enjoyed bringing people together, always liked to include every one, and liked to have a drink in good company. They said he was physically and mentally strong (he was a hard worker, achiever, and a fighter for people's rights), and had a deep spirituality. His deeper inner life sustained him. He was not egotistical (he always remained humble). They said many women pursued him (true). His spirituality and music were connected (we played in gospel bands). They said our two strong bonds were music and spiritual or religious interest. They said he was a kind, gentle, and very sensitive person. He had a big heart full of love. He could be very laid back, calm, and mellow. They said he died at an advanced age- 70s or 80s-of a heart attack. They said he was never wealthy, but never needed much in the way of material possessions. They said he appreciated what I had done for him (prolonged medical care).

They didn't get 3 direct hits. They got about 30. Their accuracy was 100%. I said, "If I didn't already believe in the afterlife, I would after this reading."

It never ceases to amaze me about how much accurate information can come through an accomplished medium. Occasionally, a piece of information that is incorrect or irrelevant will come through. No one is 100% accurate all of the time. Also, certain details, such as exact ages, numbers, and names are difficult to convey. Some mediums are especially gifted in transmitting that kind of information. Also, I have noticed how messages are often conveyed in words that are familiar to the medium or characteristic of the medium, and not always in words, expressions, or nuances the deceased would use.

I received a communication in the Bahamas through an accomplished professional medium who correctly identified my aunt. One thing she did was describe my aunt's love of gardening. But she didn't stop there. She communicated that my aunt was interested in horticulture, grafting, and genetically breeding plants. I did have a great uncle on that aunt's side who was involved in that kind of work, but my aunt wasn't. That was a lesson for me on how the medium's mind can expand on what they get and add their own thoughts or interpretation to the message.

If this can happen to a professional medium, was about me? I learned that even the more advanced mediums are subject to pitfalls and the expression, "Give what you get- don't interpret ", is good advice.

I had a chance earlier to be the medium and read for her. I was intimidated because she was a seasoned professional and I was a green beginner. I looked at her and thought, "Oh, God, please let me give an accurate reading." I started to give the information that was coming through, and every time I said something, she said, "No, no, no ". All I heard were no's and I was sinking lower and lower into the seat. I thought, "I must be a fake medium." The communicating spirit was very verbal and finally I said, "He says he was a lawyer." And she responded, "Oh, that (*#!*#!*)." Then she started to corroborate everything I had said. She wasn't expecting him to come through because they had a very unpleasant relationship. He indicated in his message that he had changed, but she wasn't ready to forgive him.

I have had a judge and a lawyer come through me. In both cases they were superb communicators and I could hear them clairaudiently. They were people who had been very verbal in their lifetime. The way in which you receive information is dependent in part on your own strengths as well as upon the strengths of the communicating spirit and how similar the two of you are. If you are energetically similar, communication will flow more freely, and if you have a strong emotional bond such as love, the flood gates can be opened.

I like to work as a "tag team ". When a medium is very experienced, such as John Edward, he can deliver a lot of information quickly. For those of us who are less developed, it is much easier to work with another medium or a group of mediums. That gives you time to get more information at a relaxed pace and it takes the pressure off when you're not in the spotlight continuously. You frequently get more information, and parts of it from each medium's unique manner of presentation. Also, some facts are easier for one medium to get than another. Each has unique strengths and weaknesses.

I recall a training session with Robert Brown in southern California. A group of us were to give and receive readings. One spirit came through and went to each one of us around the circle, giving each one of us a detail of his life that added up to a complete portrait of him. It was as though each medium was an instrument in the orchestra and the final composition was a biography of that spirit's life.

That brings me to another example like the former. I was in Florida at a spiritualist church for a special event when I got a brief reading from a medium in training. She accurately described a man, the love of my life, and said, "I get that he was a hunter." I said, "No, not that I know of ", and she said, "Well, he showed me a rifle." I said, "Oh, that makes sense because he was in the army." So that is an example of how a medium can interpret something in a different way from what the spirit intended.

Sometimes two or three spirits will come through simultaneously, particularly if they have a number of things in common. For highly developed mediums, such as Bill Collier, the Scottish medium, it is possible to juggle, or go back and forth between multiple spirits at the same time. Otherwise, the sitter may aid in this recognition. It's almost like a conference call.

At a Lisa Williams training session, I was able to bring two relatives through for a sitter at the same time. They were distinctly different, and each one politely waited as they took turns. Before the end of the reading, I knew the personality of each one well enough to know which one was speaking at any given time. I think of this as a conference call, where multiple parties are communicating at once.

My loved one in spirit has a terrific sense of humor. He gives me funny scenarios he makes up with images and dialogue. One night in the Bahamas we literally talked all night. I have never laughed so loud or had such a good time in my life. I'm glad the neighbors didn't know I was the only living occupant, because I'm sure they thought I was on my honeymoon and having a great time. I was having a great time- I missed the meditation on the beach the next morning because I was too tired to get up.

Another thing we did together was the hot tub experience. The whole group of mediums decided to lounge in the spa together that afternoon. We all got in and were laughing and joking around. The other mediums started playing and dunking each other under the water. My loved one, my partner in spirit, started to move my hands and arms in the water. It was easy because of the decreased resistance. He even flipped me over and dunked me. I came up laughing and coughing.

Later in a reading he came through with the deceased husband of another medium. The one said "honey "and the other said "moon ". That was so significant for me because every year I went to the Bahamas, my partner and I called it our honeymoon. So we had a honeymoon every year.

He also communicated to me through multiple mediums who had said they saw interlocking rings, that the ring I wear with his inscription needs to go to the other side with me, and that this is the beginning of our eternal union. I have had so much corroboration from him personally and through mediums that I can only say that although I desperately miss him here in the physical, I am forever thankful I will have his love and companionship eternally in spirit.

So many friends, acquaintances, loved ones, and relatives have come through to me. I feel exceedingly fortunate to have the knowledge of their continued survival. It gives hope and encouragement, trust and consolation. If all of the painful lessons, all the tribulation, lead me to the love, joy, and peace of the next life, my dreams will have indeed come true. How could I ever ask for more?

Some of the most beautiful comments I have ever received are from the one I love, and have been communicated through mediums. They are romantic love letters from beyond. As one medium told me, "You don't have to wait until you join him on the other side. The two of you are together now." This is the love that sustains me, the reason behind my work, my efforts, my desire for self improvement, and the foundation of my hope. It is the desire of my heart fulfilled, an eternal promise.

Thirty Two
# Spirit Guidance

Based on what has happened to me and on what other mediums have told me, we are often guided or advised by Spirit. This doesn't mean that we don't have free will. It only means that we receive suggestions or help when we need or request it.

I can recall one such situation. I travelled across the country to see a physical medium several years ago. I had never seen one before and knew there weren't too many doing public demonstrations. At least I thought I was going to see the medium. But Spirit had other plans for me.

It turned out that I was very disappointed in the demonstration because it was set up in such a way that you were completely unable to validate anything that happened. Also, a friend of mine received a very generic message from his supposed grandfather in a voice and with a speaking pattern and cadence that were not even remotely like his. No specific validating evidence was given. In the pitch darkness I was supposedly touched by a Spirit who was a famous healer in his physical lifetime. I felt small, cold, perspiring, or "clammy " hands on my forehead. I told my friend about what I felt. The next day the physical medium shook hands with my friend. He was taken aback and told me, "Oh, shit, he had small, cold, perspiring, 'clammy' hands . I couldn't believe what I felt after what you told me."

What did happen that was significant was that a very humble man, a photographer who had lost his wife, gave me a book list and told me about a website maintained by the University of Pennsylvania called Spiritwritings.com. Through the books he recommended and those I downloaded from that website, I was able to obtain a great deal of valuable information and read about personal accounts that answered some of the questions I had about the afterlife. In fact, they played a large role in inspiring me to write this book.

Many other good things resulted from that trip. That was where I first purchased the " *Karma I and II*" books by Shanna Spalding St. Clair, which have been so instructive and influential for me.

I also met another woman whose first name is Jayne, a paranormal investigator specializing in EVP's. She e-mailed me free software, including EVP maker, Audacity, and her background AM radio sweep for male and female voices, as well as a background white noise recording. With her software I was able to record my first EVP's from my deceased loved one, showing me that EVP's are real and giving me the comfort of hearing my loved one's voice.

I am very grateful for that trip, but the wonderful things I received from going were totally unexpected, and not what I went for in the first place. I feel that Spirit directed me to go for these other reasons that have played a significant role in my healing, my knowledge, my life, and my development a medium.

I have another friend, Laurie, who, as a medium, says she is guided by Spirit to attend certain conferences, read certain books, and meet certain people. She feels, too, that she is strongly guided by spirit in her development.

I have also discovered that each medium is unique and has his or her own strengths and weaknesses. Some receive their messages from hearing and can more accurately reproduce the communicating spirit's words. Others are more directly influenced by feelings and are very sensitive in delivering messages of the heart. These can be very healing to the sitter. Others are more clairvoyant and get their communication more through pictures and symbols. John Edward uses a communication system of symbols. So does Theresa Caputo, the "Long Island Medium ". For instance, seeing pink flowers is a symbol John Edward uses for spirits to convey their love, and white flowers signify a wedding or anniversary. Theresa Caputo says her symbol of two hands held together signifies that the deceased and their living loved one were together at the time of passing. You can develop your own symbols. The only thing you need to do is choose memorable symbols that you and your guides establish, are aware of, and agree upon.

Some mediums can channel spirits. They are able to temporarily suspend their own thoughts, disassociate themselves, and permit the spirits to talk or channel directly through them. This is usually done in a trance of varying degrees from light trance to deep trance. It is a letting go or relinquishment of your own control and allowing a Spirit to step in temporarily and communicate more directly through you without the interference of your conscious mind.

James Van Praagh uses this technique in training mediums. In his classes he teaches you to ask a Spirit to step near and "overlay" on you- in other words, to allow that Spirit to impress their thoughts and feelings on you so that you feel what they felt, think what they thought. You can, so to speak, say, "I feel that I am ", or "I know I was ", and deliver that spirit's message in the first person.

Some mediums stress evidential detail, which is important, because you first need to recognize and confirm that you are indeed speaking to your deceased loved one. But after you have enough evidence to firmly believe you are, other types of messages may become more important to you. That is when channeled messages or answers to specific questions you may have, become important. After I was convinced my loved one was still alive, and I was communicating with him, I wanted to know what it was like on the other side. Was he the same person I love and remember or was he different, and if so, how? What was life like on the other side and what can I look forward to when I join him?

These are questions I was able to ask and get answers to after I developed to my own mediumship and began to channel my loved one. I still can "hear "him better than I can other spirits, I guess because we are so similar in our personalities, and have such a deep bond of love.

Thirty Three

# Skepticism and Belief

As with any belief system or religion, the existence of life after death and its nature cannot be conclusively proven at this time. I have accrued enough personal evidence that I fully believe in my heart the continuation of existence after the death of the physical body. As my friend Laurie said to me, "Penny, you have your truth." So you also have your truth. What you believe is truth to you.

A relative of mine looked at it this way. "If I believe there is a life after death and I die and there isn't, what have I lost? But if I don't believe and there is a life after death, then I have lost out on a lot. I have more comfort believing that I will again see those I have loved and lost. I have more joy believing that there is a meaning in my life, a purpose, and a better life to look forward to. That is why I choose to believe."

In my first training session, I was in the Bahamas in an advanced mediumship training class with Robert Brown. I had just received my first reading from him after the loss of my loved one and will always be grateful to him, for I feel that he "saved my life". When the reading was nearly over he asked me if I would be interested in participating in a class in mediumship and said that even if someone participates in training for selfish reasons, they can still be used by spirit to help others. I was nervous and scared, but I jumped at the opportunity.

Here I was, a complete beginner in a class with highly developed mediums. All I can say is that spirit helped me. When I got up on the platform in front of the audience, the correct words were given to me and I was able to give accurate and acceptable readings to others. Robert said that spirit was giving me a huge pile of gifts and presents and it was up to me which ones I would keep and which I would give away.

During that class Robert lead us through an exercise of speed reading, in which half of us were sitters and the other half were mediums. We were given 5 minutes at each station and rotated through the whole group. I was one of the sitters. When I got to the last station, a former acquaintance, who had been a professor and a physician, came through with specific evidential details of his life, illness, and our relationship. The details fit exactly with him and with no one else I had known. I recognized that it was him immediately. However, the most interesting part was the reference I got last to a conversation we had had shortly before he died. He was a skeptic and a non-believer. I had told him at the time that there was another life after death. He remained a doubter. The last thing the medium said to me was, "The conversation the two of you had before he died- he says, you were right." Combined with all the other details, this was the most telling.

My mother, despite the fact that my grandmother was a medium, had a healthy degree of skepticism until later in her life. She wasn't as interested in mediumship and the afterlife as I was. I do remember her saying, "If we die and never have the opportunity to see the ones we love again, what is life worth in the first place?" My mother was very close to her sister. When her sister was at Mayo Clinic undergoing an operation for removal of a lung nodule, my mother was very worried. While she was staying overnight at my cousin's house, she was lying in bed hoping for the best. She later told me that she felt someone tap her on the shoulder, and then the lights went on by themselves in the dark bedroom where she was lying on the bed. She felt she was being given a sign from her mother, my grandmother, who had passed, that everything was going to be alright.

Another incident that persuaded my mother about the reality of the afterlife occurred right after my grandmother died. The whole family was staying overnight in my mother's home in Florida. There weren't enough beds to accommodate everyone so my cousin was sleeping on the couch in the living room. It was late and everyone had just gotten to bed. It was about 2:00 o'clock in the morning. Suddenly, the lights in the family room began to blink on and off repeatedly by themselves. My cousin began to scream and other members of the family had also seen them blinking. My mother and I both felt that was my grandmother communicating with us that she was still alive and okay.

When I was young and in college I was always seeking greater understanding about life and about the possibility of an afterlife. I took courses in comparative religion and bought books investigating ESP and the afterlife. I had spoken with the man who was Chairman of the department of religion at the college I attended about my interests. He was a traditional thinker and very conservative. He did introduce me to a man who had been a former priest and instructor at a local university. That man's name was Dr. Fehring. He also was interested in mysticism and life after death. I gained much wisdom from him and long past his death the things I learned from him have remained influential in my life. After he passed, I received communications from him through my mediumistic grandmother. I received very specific details pertinent to him and our relationship, including a favorite name he had for me, which no one, including my grandmother, ever knew.

Later on I had the opportunity to speak with the Chairman of the department of religion who had introduced me to Dr. Fehring. At that time he had undergone some significant life trauma and the loss of loved ones. He, who had been a skeptic previously, now asked me to write up a paper on my after death communications with Dr. Fehring. I did this and sent it to him. I noted how sometimes it takes a painful loss for people to consider the possibility of life after death and inquire about it.

What I can tell you is that I always was interested in that possibility and felt that understanding my life and the meaning of life in general was very important to me. I was a seeker of truth. It is the specific incidents of communication through my grandmother and now through many other mediums that have persuaded me completely that our lives continue. Without that very personal evidence I could only have believed, but now I have an assurance in my heart that no one can take away.

Thirty Four

# War Stories

I have decided to include several other episodes that have happened that are important to me. I call them war stories because they are memorable things that I fondly recall.

The Tarot card: When I first started attending a development circle, I had my first introduction to Tarot cards. I had never seen one before. We used them as a focal point or inspiration for a mediumship reading. In the exercises, we each had to draw a card from which our partner would give a reading. I had just lost the love of my life through death. We had made vows to one another to remain united eternally. It seemed more than coincidental that the first card I ever chose showed a picture of a man with his arms around a woman, looking down at her, and the inscription on the card was, "eternal union ". That reading, which I received from a lovely, vibrant medium in her 80s, was a beautiful confirmation of what my loved one and I had previously discussed.

The possession: When I relate this incident it is not referring to a serious, frightening possession, but a light hearted incident that occurred which I will never forget. I should preface this incident with a discussion of some techniques I learned from the renowned medium, James Van Praagh. I took a recent class from him where he taught us how to let a spirit overshadow us or blend/merge with us while we are giving a reading. He said that giving a message and communicating with a loved one should be a joyous occasion, not just a serious one. Several people who volunteered to get up and give platform readings did just that. In addition to giving evidential details to establish the identity of the spirit, they all requested the spirit to convey his or her personality to them. When they did this, they began to give colorful, lively depictions of the spirit's personality and character. In essence, they temporarily became the spirit, acting and talking or behaving like the spirits did when they were alive. This added a whole new wonderful dimension to the reading. We didn't get "just the facts, ma'am ", but we got a vivid picture of who the spirit was when they were alive.

That was when the humor came through. The spirits who came through made us laugh by showing us their former identities, illustrating their faults and their idiosyncrasies.

This leads me to the story about what happened in spirit circle. That wonderful lady I described earlier who was a former schoolteacher, now in her 80s, and had lost her own husband, brought through my loved one and started to act like him. She said, "Penny, I just want to give you a hug and a kiss. It's not me talking, it's him." She then started to laugh and said, "He's possessing me." We both laughed and I got a beautiful message that I cherish.

Klassina and the dog: On one of my trips to the Bahamas, one of Robert Brown's training sessions, a friend of my friend, Laurie, was there. She was from the Netherlands and had come all that way for training. Being typical students, although we were supposed to conserve our energy for the class, we decided to do some mischief and have a circle reading in our hotel room at night. I will never forget the reading that Klassina gave to me. She began to bring through my dog, who had been dead for a number of years. I loved the dog as others would love a child. This dog was exceptionally intelligent and we had a very close bond. As she brought through details of the dog's appearance and behavior, she also said, "The dog is doing something odd with its nose. It's scrunching it up like this." She began to wiggle and twist her nose like the dog did. This was a very clean dog, and I used to kiss her on the nose, just like the medium depicted. That was quite a specific reading for me.

Book confirmations: I have had 3 different readings from different mediums in different parts of the country confirming that I should write this book. I had always been a reader and a writer, and I wanted to share the experiences that have given me such joy and hope with others. The first was from a very good medium named Lisa who suggested that I write a book. I had already been thinking of doing this. The second confirmation came in a class I took given by Lisa Williams, the well known medium who has published books and had her own television show. On the last day of the class, she brought in some members of the general public for us to give readings to.

I gave readings to a young man and a young lady. I brought through details regarding their relatives who had passed and details of their current lives that I would have no way of knowing. At the end of each reading I said to each sitter, "Is there any question you would like to ask before the session ends?" At that time I was planning on writing the book and had two separate main topics in mind. The first was providing answers to a question I had always had- what is the afterlife like? The second was about something that happened to me that I thought could also help others. That was how we each can attempt to develop mediumship and communication with our own lost loved ones if we desire.

When I got to the end of the first reading and asked the young man, "Do you have any questions," he said, "How can I communicate, myself, with my loved ones who have crossed over?" I thought, "This is interesting", because this is one of the very questions I had been planning on addressing in the book. After I finished the second reading, I asked the young lady if she had any questions. She said, "Yes, I was wondering, what is the afterlife like?" This clinched it for me. I thought, two sitters, and each one has asked the very questions I planned on discussing in the book.

The third confirmation I got was from a new young medium at James Van Praagh's recent class. She brought through my former dog that I had when I was growing up. She had no idea I was in the process of writing a book. She said, the dog is wiggling and very excited. It wants you to continue the writing you are doing, and if you publish it in a book, it will be successful."

I do know multiple mediums have brought through animals from the afterlife. I have been told that we have greater communication with them there and continue to have relationships with those animals we have loved and who have loved us. Whether a dog can understand what it is to write a book I don't know. Assuredly, I will some day. In either case, this was a third confirmation for me about the book I was writing from yet a third person who had no idea I was writing a book.

As I was writing this passage, I read a newsletter from a well known medium on the West Coast, Hollister Rand. She is the author of a book she wrote to help grieving parents who have lost children called, "*I'm Not Dead, I'm Different*". In her newsletter, she happened to be discussing animal communications, and responds to the question a man once posed to her, "How can animals speak English?" She replies that many animals have communicated to her in words, pictures, feelings, and sounds. She cites the research with the gorilla, "Coco", who used sign language to communicate difficult concepts with her trainers. I discussed this with a friend of mine who is a good medium. We conjectured that perhaps the animals were able to convey ideas, which were translated into English words by the mind of the medium. My dog certainly seemed able to understand concepts and language to a surprising degree. I often used to say she understood the same amount of vocabulary as a five year old child. She just lacked the proper vocal cords and physiologic equipment to express herself in words. If this was true, who is to say animals couldn't convey a thought which the medium translates into words?

The animal lovers: Before I began training as a medium, myself, I was despondent about the loss of the dog that was so close to me. She had died at the age of 18, a ripe old age for a dog. She was exceptionally smart. One time during medical school while I was lying on the bed studying , my dog curled up on my books. I didn't change my tone of voice or gesture to her to move, I just said, "Oh, honey, mama's gotta work." She immediately got up and walked down to the foot of the bed, where she lay down. Although they say dogs cannot understand abstract concepts, I used to say to my dog, "Honey, what do you want? Tell me what you want." She was able to extrapolate that the question, "What do you want?" had multiple answers. Sometimes she would go to the refrigerator wanting food and sometimes she would go to the door wanting to go outside. Other times she would go to the bed wanting to get up on the bed.

After she passed, I went to a group reading given by John Edward, the well known medium from television, hoping that I would hear from her. I didn't hear from her at that time, but an interesting phenomenon did occur. I sat in a particular row on the right side of the demonstration room in the front. I guess this is what you call synchronicity, something that seems to be more than just coincidence. I later found out that everyone in that row had lost a pet they were hoping to hear from. John gave a reading to a man and woman in the audience, describing their relationship with the child they had lost. He said, "This is unusual. I see you rubbing your child's stomach. Did your child have a problem with its stomach?" They said, "No. We had a dog that we loved like a child and we always rubbed his stomach." Even though the species was different, the love was the same.

The clown: I have been to other interesting readings. One was a development circle that a friend of mine attended. On that occasion, a man came through for him who had been a good friend and had done a great deal of charitable work in his lifetime as a clown donating time entertaining sick children in hospitals. He came through successively to each member of the circle, giving each one a different aspect of his life and experience. When my friend went home he looked up his friend on the Internet, and found that indeed, he had died three months prior to the reading. In this case, each medium was able to contribute information that added to the big picture of the spirit's life. Sometimes a reading like this can be very rewarding, as each medium is contacting the same spirit and getting evidential detail separately that accurately describes the same spirit. For each one of these mediums to receive something different and appropriate to the spirit's life and character is even more evidential. Each one provides a piece of the jigsaw puzzle, building up a portrait of who the spirit was. One of the mediums remarked, "He's not just funny, he's a real clown, with all the makeup and a costume."

He was making all these mediums, who had never known him, laugh, as he had done with people in life.

One of the readings I gave at Lisa Williams' class involved bringing through two spirits at the same time. I have since learned that this is a technique some mediums like to develop. My friends, Kari and Laurie, attended a teaching session with the Scottish medium, Bill Collier, and they told me he asked students to bring through several spirits at once, alternating between them. This is what happened to me during one of my readings. The young man I was reading for had two relatives that came through, one from each side of the family. At first it was confusing, but they were very polite, each waiting his turn. I was going back and forth between them and before the end of the reading I was able to tell which one was speaking just by their very different personalities and characteristics.

In one reading given to me at a teaching seminar hosted by James Van Praagh several years ago, a medium in training brought through my great-grandfather. I had never met him in my lifetime, but I knew him by family stories and by pictures. He came through with the appearance and details of his life that I would recognize. In his life he was a very successful business owner. He had a very traditional concept of the role of women in the business world, which was common in his time. He made the statement that in his lifetime he thought that women were not able to match arms with men or to succeed as equals in the business world. He gave me a pat on the back for the success I achieved in my career. This would be an appropriate statement from him, for whether he believed this in the afterlife or not, this is how he felt when he was alive, and was highly characteristic of the way he thought, identifying him. It was also a huge compliment to me.

Happy Trails to You: I was looking through my television guide when I noticed a paranormal investigation show about CCPI, Central California Paranormal Investigators. Several of the guest investigators were members of a group called the Lightworkers. They lived in my general area, and when I found out that one of them was hosting an open mediumship development circle about an hour from my home, I decided to attend. One Saturday afternoon I went. There was a group of about 35 or 40 people none of whom I knew except for the friend who came with me. We were informed that we were going to give readings for one of the sitters, who had recently suffered the loss of a loved one. She was a complete stranger to me.

When my turn came to give her a reading, in addition to other details I received, I heard the song Happy Trails to You, the old Roy Rogers and Dale Evans theme song. I've since learned not to question myself when things like this come to me because I've learned that, however improbable they seem to me, they often have a very personal meaning for the sitter. When I said that the woman began to cry and said, "My husband's name was Dale Evans, and he often was teased about it with the song you just mentioned."

I have also heard that the communications we have with spirit are a two way street. While the earth is our school and we are learning lessons in our earth lives, as well as being guided by spirit, those who have crossed over do not instantly become perfect or omniscient. They continue to learn on the other side and are learning with us. If they had to address a certain issue in their life, they may observe someone on earth who is facing that same issue to learn how others cope with that type of problem. So it seems we are all learning together from one another. We can teach and heal spirits on the other side, as they can also teach and heal us.

I am very grateful for all the experiences I have had, appreciative of my guides and the many loved ones who have come through for me and for others, as well as the many other mediums who have brought loved ones through or taught me. These are the experiences that have made me who I am and have given me comfort and hope for the future, both in this life, and the next one.

Thirty Five

# House Cleansings, Guides, and Déjà vu

A friend of mine was preparing to do a house cleansing. The family was ready to give up and move. They had experienced spirit activity in their home for years, and were becoming more and more unnerved. They had had prior house cleansings from several paranormal investigative groups and two exorcisms performed by Catholic priests. None of these had rid the home of spirits.

The night before the house cleansing my friend asked for a guide who specialized in protection to help her the day of the cleansing. She channeled a guide, who came through in automatic writing, calling himself Alexander, and stating that he had been a flyer in the great war and was Prussian. He stated that he was a defender and protector and would be there to help her when she went in for the cleansing. She was able to draw him through spirit art, and said he was in a uniform with epaulets on his shoulders and had a mustache. She said there were details including medals on his uniform. He spoke with confidence and authority.

We wondered if we could find a record of such a person on the Internet. I did find a Prince Alexander Frederick, a Prussian flyer from World War II, and wonder if that is him.

We do have a master guide who remains with us from birth through death. We also have other guides who step in periodically to help us with a particular problem or specialty. Sometimes a loved one or relative may step in to guide as well, as we often will listen and respond more readily to a loved one we have known in our lifetime.

There are meditations which can help us contact, communicate, and learn of our spirit guides if we don't know them already.

When my friend went to do the house cleansing she encountered the spirit of an elderly woman who had had an accident in the bathroom while she was alive and was causing some disturbance in the home to draw attention to herself. My friend spoke with the spirit and the family, giving them guidance and therapeutic help. Oftentimes spirits can benefit from counseling as people can. Families who have experienced paranormal activity can be fearful, and counseling about the spirit world and how to exert their own power in a loving manner can be of benefit.

With that help, the family was able to help the spirit cross over.

Ghosts can have issues, too. If spirits knew everything, they wouldn't need to reincarnate on earth to learn. It is interesting that we on earth are learning, but that spirits can learn too. In fact, we can learn together and discuss choices together. It is a give and take.

Just as the spirits can discuss the "what if's" of their lives and conjecture about what may have been a better choice than the one they made or what they would choose to do if they could live over again with the knowledge they now have, we can discuss issues, think things out, and draw conclusions together.

We on earth are somewhat like a laboratory where spirits can look at how others cope with issues they themselves once faced. We are all continuously learning.

One interesting facet of the cleansing was the incident in which the wife woke up one morning and found her shoes stretched out. It was explained that the spirit had loved clothing and shoes and in her thoughts had manifested a physical effect upon the shoes. This may seem farfetched, but two others describe this same effect.

One is William Buhlman. He is known for his experiments with astral projection. He is a well known author, and I took a course from him at the Monroe Institute in Virginia.

He said that when traveling on the astral plane you have to be careful because your thoughts create your environment and circumstances with an immediacy unknown on earth. He said that if you think of or concentrate on something, it appears. In other words, thoughts manifest directly as reality without the intervention of builders.

Another related example is from a book by another astral projector, this time from England, Frederick Sculthorpe. He had lost his dearly beloved wife and began astrally projecting to see her. He described a situation on the astral plane in which he saw two spirits fighting, and one kicked the other. Spirits do not have human bodies and, as such, do not have physical pain. But the spirit's remembrance of physical pain, his anticipation of pain, and his recall of what the pain felt like if someone had kicked him on earth, caused him to "feel "pain. This is another example of thoughts manifesting directly in reality- the sense of pain.

Déjà vu is another interesting topic. My friend, who died after being in a coma at the age of 25 and was revived, had the experience of talking with his uncle while he was in the coma. He found out later from his mother that the conversation had occurred several weeks after his uncle died. He also described being out of his body after he died, watching them revive him from a corner of the room. He saw all of the proceedings and was able to tell the doctor later exactly what happened in great detail after he died.

That same friend has had multiple instances of déjà vu. He has walked into buildings knowing exactly where outlets and electrical equipment were located despite never having been in those buildings in his lifetime. He also was born with an uncanny ability to build and repair things and a strong mechanical aptitude. He describes having taken the locks apart upstairs in his home at the age of 5 and putting them back together after his mother admonished him, "You'd better put those back together before your father gets home ."

The television series, "The Ghost Inside My Child ", is interesting. I do believe some children have detailed recall of prior past life experiences that they would have no way of knowing at a young age in this lifetime. I, myself, recall no particular past lives, but do have a very strong sense that the one I love on the other side is "the man I have loved forever ".

Thirty Six
# Postscript

Here are several commentaries from my guide.
My guide's commentary on those who have crossed over versus ghosts:

> "We don't want to scare, harm, or upset people. It is much more difficult for us to be heard, seen, or felt by those remaining on the earth once we have crossed over. We have transitioned to a higher vibrational level than those spirits remaining near the earth, and it takes much more effort for us to manifest ourselves in a manner that can be recognized physically. If we have a special need to help or contact someone, we can get the help of collective energy from other spirits and guides. We have to learn to manifest ourselves in the physical. It takes considerable energy and effort. It is more difficult if we have crossed over as our vibrational energy is higher and less like that of the earth."

My guide's commentary on mediumship:

"We are not gone. We are just in a different form. We have the ability to hear the ones we have left behind. I'm not so much in a different space as a different dimension. We can still be with those we love and aware of their lives. When I am with you, I know what you are thinking and am able to communicate what I think. We can let you know things. We all have some difficulty when we are communicating because of the doubt, or the personality and the preoccupations of the medium. We need to overcome the thoughts of the medium to convey ours. It's like an intermeshing of thoughts. We use words that the medium is aware of, and we need to communicate and express ourselves when the medium is not thinking. Otherwise you get what the medium thinks, not what we think. We have different abilities to do this depending on how accomplished we are. We also will have to be aware of the medium's sensitivities, strengths, and abilities. It is a merger of both."

My guide's general comments about life on the other side:

"We live like we want to. We don't have the ability to hurt others. We have a more peaceful existence. It's a better life than we had before, not filled with unhappiness. We have the same type of personality we had but just without the body. We don't do many of the things we did on earth because they are no longer necessary. Those things we did to support our body- eating, sleeping are no longer relevant. It's more like a happy vacation without the cares and worries . We do what we love and love what we do.

We do maintain friendships and relationships. We do not harm and are not harmed. We have greater understanding, awareness, and sight. We see, hear, and touch, but not in the manner we did when in the body. It is a more ideal life. We do learn and work at improving ourselves.

We are a discrete energy, a consciousness, a personality that is able to be manifested in different forms. We know we are the same person we were, but with the greater awareness of our past. We are aware of our feelings and thoughts without subterfuge, or deceit. Our true character is known. We know the true feelings, thoughts, and acts of those we interacted with or were close to on earth, as they know ours. No one is deceived and things are not hidden. No one makes decisions based on false pretenses. Honesty prevails.

We do have free will and choice and are with those we are happy and comfortable with. We don't bear ill will toward those who hurt us or those we were unhappy with on earth. We learn the lesson in the experience and don't dwell on the past. We move on and live our lives, going in separate directions. We don't stay with people we are or were unhappy with or incompatible with. We respect their path, what we learned from the relationship, and continue on ours.

People who have the deepest bond and love for one another are the ones who remain together. Most of us have paths that cross, but if we love someone deeply, we can remain with them, even for eternity.

We don't have loss. We don't have grief. We don't have troubles or pain. We live in a more caring, loving, environment with those we love. It's not something to be afraid of. It is something to look forward to. It's the life you would have wanted if you could have chosen it. It's my idea of a happy, fulfilled existence.

You are drawn to a level according to what you demonstrated on earth, creating your own destiny. You cannot measure the happiness we have and the love that we feel. It is beyond anything we knew in the body. Our lives are so much happier we don't miss the earth, only those we love who remain. Nothing will be lost, things will only be added. We don't lose, we gain. This is a wonderful place. We take with us our knowledge, our memories, and, most importantly, our love, for true love never ends or dies. What we experience is based upon what we were like, how we conducted our lives, what we think, feel, and desire.

Be not afraid. No one loses their life- only the outside shell, and comes home richer for the difficulties they endured and the lessons they learned. We have more abundant life, greater happiness, and everlasting love."

General comments from my guide:

"We are not unhappy on this side. We have many things that people on earth don't have. We have full control of our thoughts and we don't need to worry about things as we did on earth. I am not different from who I was when I was alive. I am not going to be a prognosticator and say that I know everything. But we are able to see things much more clearly. I am going to be a much better person since I have come to realize my own errors. We all need to look at ourselves when we are judging others. We do not look at things like we did. We are able to look at the larger picture.

Tell them that no one ever dies. We don't lose our life. We simply conform to a new body. We don't live like we did with all of the unhappiness, worry, suffering, loss, struggle, dissension, and violence. We are much more at peace. We are all living in a much better place.

We have our own choices. Those who are similar in thought and desire are together. There are so many things in the afterlife that no one will ever want for anything. It is all of our finest dreams come true. We have the desires of our hearts, as long as having those desires does not harm others.

Now we are able to communicate with others we have left behind. We have that ability. I would say this. No one ever need worry about the ones they have lost. We are here and waiting for you with our arms open and our hearts full of love. No one will ever part those who love one another. When you are ready to join us we will be there with you, and meet you with joy, as one who is born into a new life."

With love,

Your guide

# Bibliography

Bethards, Betty, *There Is No Death*, (Petaluma, California: New Century, 2007) (Original Work Published 1977)

Borgia, Anthony, *Life in the World Unseen*, (Kindle Edition, 2009) (Original Work Published 1954)

Brown, Robert, *We Are Eternal*, (New York: Warner Books, 2003)

Cummins, Geraldine, *The Road to Immortality*, (Norfolk, England: Thetford, 1984) (Original Work Published 1932)

Cummins, Geraldine, *Beyond Human Personality*, (London, England: Psychic Press, 1935)

Cummins, Geraldine, *Travelers in Eternity*, (London, England: Knapp, Drewett & Sons, 1948)

Dresser, Charlotte & Rafferty, Fred, *Life Here and Hereafter*, (San Jose, California: Cosmos, 1927)

Dresser, Charlotte & Rafferty, Fred, *Spirit World and Spirit Life*, (Kindle Edition, 2010) (Original Work Published 1922)

Farr, Sidney Saylor, *What Tom Sawyer Learned from Dying*, (Norfolk, Virginia: Hampton Roads, 1993)

Kelway-Bamber, L., *Claude's Second Book*, (Whitefish, Montana: Kessinger, 2010) (Original Work Published 1920)

Lodge, Oliver, & Lodge, Raymond, *Raymond or Life and Death, Vol. I and II*, (Kindle Edition, 2011) (Original Work Published 1916)

Monroe, Robert, *Journeys Out of the Body*, (New York: Broadway Books, 2001) (Original Work Published 1971)

Scott, John, *As One Ghost to Another*, (London, England: Spiritualist Press, 1948)

Sculthorpe, Frederick C., *Excursions to the Spirit World*, (London, England: The Greater World Association, 1961)

St. Clair, Shanna Spalding, *Karma I and II, (no location provided: S. C. Walter, 1993)*

Swain, Jasper, *On the Death of My Son*, (Northhamptonshire, England: The Aquarian Press, 1974)

Williams, Lisa, *Survival of the Soul*, (Carlsbad, California: Hayhouse, 2011)

Winninger, Toni Ann, *Life Lessons*, (Lake Bluff, Illinois: Celestial Voices, 2012)

Winninger, Toni Ann, *Talking with Leaders of the Past*, (Lake Bluff, Illinois: Celestial Voices, 2008)

Winninger, Toni Ann, *Talking with Twentieth Century Men*, (Lake Bluff, Illinois: Celestial Voices, 2008)

Vogel, Gretchen, *Choices in the Afterlife*, (Keene, New Hampshire: Choices Publishing, 2010)

www.ingramcontent.com/pod-product-compliance
Lightning Source LLC
Chambersburg PA
CBHW061303110426
42742CB00012BA/2034